# CONTENTS

# Mark Hitchcock

# 2012
## The Bible
### and the
### End of the World

HARVEST HOUSE PUBLISHERS

EUGENE, OREGON

**2012, THE BIBLE, AND THE END OF THE WORLD**
Copyright © 2009 by Mark Hitchcock
Published by Harvest House Publishers
Eugene, Oregon 97402
www.harvesthousepublishers.com

Library of Congress Cataloging-in-Publication Data
  Hitchcock, Mark.
  2012, the Bible, and the end of the world / Mark Hitchcock.
    p. cm.
  ISBN 978-0-7369-2651-5 (pbk.)
  1. End of the world—Biblical teaching. 2. Bible—Prophecies—End of the world. 3. Maya calendar—Miscellanea.
4. Mayas—Prophecies. I. Title.
BS649.E63H565 2009
236.'9—dc22

                                                                          2009021399

**Printed in the United States of America**

09 10 11 12 13 14 15 16 17 / VP-NI / 10 9 8 7 6 5 4 3 2

*To Samuel*

*Thanks for helping me research the material for this book. I will never forget the summer we spent together.*

*You are a wise, faithful son who "makes a father glad" (Proverbs 10:1).*

# A.D. 2012

"Never before has a date in history been so significant to so many cultures, so many religions, scientists, and governments."

"The Mayan calendar is at the center of a cultural phenomenon. To some, 2012 will bring the end of time; to
others, it carries the promise of a new beginning; to still
others, 2012 provides an explanation for troubling new
realities—environmental change, for example—that
seem to be beyond the control of our technology and
impervious to reason. Just in time for the final five-year
countdown, the Mayan apocalypse has come of age."

THE NEW YORK TIMES
JULY 1, 2007

# INTRODUCTION

In 2007 I was watching a news program in which a journalist was interviewing a scientist about the coming "end of the world" in 2012. As a serious student of Bible prophecy and eschatology (the study of last things), the discussion quickly grabbed my attention. A brief search of "2012" on the Internet opened up a new world to me. I suddenly realized that there is an apocalyptic subculture that seriously believes the world is going to end in 2012 and that this subculture has flooded into the mainstream. Web sites, articles, books, YouTube videos, and even major motion pictures are spreading the message of an imminent apocalypse.

It immediately became clear to me that I needed to understand what all the hoopla is about—why December 21, 2012 has been targeted as earth's expiration date, and what people are expecting to happen. This book is the fruit of that search.

The tagline for the movie *2012* is "Find out the truth…if you dare." I invite you to join me in taking this dare—to join me in an investigation of the evidence for whether the world will end in 2012, to find out if there's any credence to the Mayan calendar theories about 12.21.12, and to search what the ancient prophecies of the Bible say about the end of days.

Mark Hitchcock
Edmond, Oklahoma
May 2009

# 12.21.12—
# THE END OF THE WORLD
# AS WE KNOW IT?

## Has the Final Countdown Begun?

"The prophecies of Nostradamus, Edgar Cayce, the Aztecs, the Hopi, the Maya, and others have sent reverberations of an unmistakable message throughout time. Separated by hundreds of years of history and thousand of miles of distance, all point to now."

GREGG BRADEN (*FRACTAL TIME*)

"The 2012 deadline is the first time in modern history when so much is on the line for so many...The year 2012 has the mark of destiny upon it."

LAWRENCE E. JOSEPH (*APOCALYPSE 2012*)

Over the last few years, Americans have been bombarded with one huge concept that can be summed up by one little word: *change.* Both major political parties, and most Americans, recognize that major adjustments are needed in the economy, education, and health care. If one is to believe the political pundits, big changes are on the way. But few people are prepared for another kind of change that many are predicting—a change they believe has been bearing down on the planet for 5000 years, the colossal transformation of our solar system and our collective psyche that many say will happen on December 21, 2012.

Many believe that ancient prophecies indicate that change is coming. Big change. Predictions vary widely about what will happen. They range from total, all-out apocalypse to some kind of quantum shift in human awareness and consciousness. Yet they all agree that big change is coming for planet earth and the human race. And they all appear to focus on one specific year—2012. And in some cases even one specific day—December 21, 2012. Their conclusion, after gathering all the prophetic material, is simple: All the ancient sources agree the world will end in 2012. After all, they say, it can't be sheer coincidence that so many primitive diviners, psychics, and astrologers agree. The bottom line is clear: Never before have so many people from diverse backgrounds and viewpoints pinpointed one day as the expiration date for human civilization.

## Signs of the Times

People everywhere seem to share a collective sense that the world is getting near closing time. Apocalyptic thinking is in the air. According to the Pew Research Foundation, about one in five Americans believes that Christ will return in the current generation.[1] A *U.S. News & World Report* poll revealed that 60 percent of all Americans, from all faith backgrounds, believe the world will end eventually. And about 20 percent say earth's life expectancy is just a couple of decades.[2] *Newsmax* observes: "If you mix the morning headlines into the average American's eschatology, you stir up a powerful, angst-inducing brew."[3]

Crises of alarming complexity are emerging and accelerating with frightening regularity—depletion of vital resources, a peak in oil production, food shortages, nuclear threats, economic meltdowns, vanishing species, potentially pandemic flu viruses, wars and rumors of wars, turmoil in the Middle East, record tsunamis, erratic weather patterns, unprecedented earthquakes, and the escalation of catastrophic storms. Life on planet earth over the last few years has been anything but business as usual. We live in a fragile, increasingly dangerous, interdependent world. We are seeing an amazing confluence of tipping points. And the world's problems are multiplying. Is this all a buildup to some imminent cataclysm? The prelude to a grand finale of unspeakable destruction? Is 2012 the year the cosmic clock winds down to zero? A time of epic disaster? Was the warning of the earth's demise indeed encoded in the Mayan calendar?

December 21, 2012 marks the end of the 5000-year cycle by the Mayan long count calendar. Were these ancient timekeepers giving us the time code for the end of days? A growing number of people are predicting that December 21, 2012 is the apocalypse deadline—history's final day. The stroke of midnight. The galactic tipping point. The astronomical Grand Finale.

But haven't we heard all this before? Setting dates for the end of the world is nothing new. There's a long, tragic history of date-setting for the end of the world. But could 2012 be different? Or is it just another hoax to scare people and rake in a few dollars?

## The Real Y2K?

You may remember Y2K. Many people were predicting that when the earth's odometer rolled over from December 31, 1999 to

January 1, 2000, we would experience all kinds of massive computer malfunctions, government shutdowns, ensuing chaos, and even the end of civilization as we know it. I remember it well. Many were caught up in the frenzy of preparing bomb shelters and storing up enough dried foods and fresh water to last for months. One of my neighbors had a compound on some property he owned outside the city where he had enough dried foods, water, fuel, generators, and guns stored to support and protect his family for years to come. I always wondered what he did with all that stuff on January 2, 2000. One example of the Y2K hysteria comes from Gary North's highly trafficked Web site:

> *We've got a problem.* It may be the biggest problem that the modern world has ever faced. I think it is. At 12 midnight on January 1, 2000 (a Saturday morning), most of the world's mainframe computers will either shut down or begin spewing out bad data. Most of the world's desktop computers will also start spewing out bad data. Tens of millions—possibly hundreds of millions—of pre-programmed computer chips will begin to shut down the systems they automatically control. This will create a nightmare for every area of life, in every region of the industrialized world.[4]

North's Web site had links to more than 3000 places where you could read similar doom-and-gloom predictions about the Y2K crisis. He grimly told visitors to his Web site that they had better heed these doomsday warnings, or they would certainly regret it. He said,

> It took me from early 1992 until late 1996 to come to grips emotionally with the Year 2000 Problem. You had better be a lot faster on the uptake than I was. We're running out of time. I don't mean that society is running

out of time to fix this problem. Society has *already* run out of time for that. There are not enough programmers to fix it. The technical problems cannot be fixed on a system-wide basis. The Millennium Bug *will* hit in 2000, no matter what those in authority decide to do now. As a system, the world economy is now beyond the point of no return. So, when I say "we," I mean you and I as individuals. We are running out of time as individuals to evade the falling dominoes...We are facing a breakdown of civilization if the power grid goes down.[5]

Of course, nothing out of the ordinary happened on January 1, 2000. The new millennium came in with a whimper, not a roar, and as expected, very few, if any, of the prophets of doom admitted they were wrong or apologized to the millions they led astray. So could it be that the whole 2012 thing is just another case of Y2K insanity? Or is it the real thing?

Serious 2012 watchers are calling 12.21.12 the "Mayan Y2K" or the "Real Y2K." It's even been called "A Y2K for the New Age."[6] Those who are 2012 believers maintain that Y2K was just a warm-up or dress rehearsal for the real show. They contend that momentous change (there's that word again), an era of quantum transformation, is coming at the winter solstice for the northern hemisphere in the year 2012.

Fueling the hype is the fact that December 21, 2012 falls on the winter solstice and allegedly marks the first time in more than 26,000 years that the galactic alignment of the sun and the earth with the center of the Milky Way Galaxy will occur. Many believe this crossing of the great galactic equator could cause the earth's poles to reverse, which would obviously be a very bad thing.

For some people, December 21, 2012 spells doomsday with disaster scenarios including volcanic eruptions caused by solar storms, massive earthquakes, cracks in the earth's magnetic field, and mass extinction brought on by a nuclear winter. Predictions abound of extreme weather pounding the planet and of the eruption of supervolcanoes, which are as powerful as 1000 Hiroshima-type atomic bombs.[7]

For others, 2012 marks the opportunity for a new beginning, a new phase of human growth, or what they sometimes call "The Shift." And for many, 2012 helps provide answers for all kinds of unsettling developments ranging from hurricanes, floods, and the disappearance of bees.

## 2012 Hits the Mainstream

For several years there's been a burgeoning apocalyptic subculture that has been warning the world about a coming catastrophe in 2012. The man who put 2012 "on the map" is José Arguelles, who authored a book in 1987 titled *The Mayan Factor*. He also established the Harmonic Convergence in 1987. It was a peace initiative that occurred on August 16-17, 1987. People all over the world gathered at allegedly sacred sites to awaken the "energy grid" and bring in a 25-year era of spiritual growth that will culminate in 2012. For Arguelles, "2012 is a marker, a wake-up call in our DNA," and the cycle will culminate during June-December 2012. After the Harmonic Convergence, the 2012 apocalyptic subculture began to emerge. They began a 25-year countdown to 2012. The 2012 movement has remained under the radar for almost 20 years, but has suddenly exploded into the mainstream. Many people today are what's being called "2012 curious." And we can expect this curiosity to grow exponentially as the date draws near. A whole new area of study known as 2012ology has erupted, and 2012 conferences are being held all over the world. According to many, "a gold rush of '2012ology' is underway."[8]

The first major conference on 2012 was held in Hollywood on March 1, 2008. Another conference, with about 300 attendees from as far away as Europe, was held at the Fort Mason Center in San Francisco on November 1-2, 2008. It was dubbed the Shift by the Bay, and the conference's slogan was: "Shift happens." The conference organizer, Christian John Meoli, plans to schedule twelve 2012 conferences in various places around the globe to prepare for the big day. According to Meoli, the final grand hurrah conference will be held appropriately on December 12, 2012, and is scheduled to take place on site at the Mayan pyramids. Everything about the conferences focuses on 2012. In fact, the entry fee at one of the conferences was…$20.12!

Describing one of these conferences, the *Los Angeles Times* reports:

> In these times of economic distress, participants shelled out $300 each to attend the sold-out 2012 Conference, where astrologers, UFO fans, shamans, and New Age entrepreneurs of every stripe presented their dreams and dreads in two days of lectures, group meditations, documentaries and, of course, self-promotion. Normally, New Age platforms attract the interest of only the narrowest group of enthusiasts. But this one has been generating wider audiences because it so forcefully underscores the turmoil of the times, as indicated by the stock market plunge, Iran's nuclear ambitions, the Sept. 11 attacks, global warming and the possibility of a magnetic pole shift and stronger sunspot cycles.[9]

All the mounting crises in the world are feeding the popular notion that the end may be near.

## You Might Want to Circle This Date on Your Calendar

In 2008, 16 percent of Americans answered yes when asked, "Do you expect any apocalyptic events to happen on December 21, 2012?"[10] That's one out of every eight Americans. And that was before there was very much information available about 2012. Just wait until movies about 2012 and television programs about the end of days begin to flood into the popular culture. That number will surely go up. People everywhere are going to be talking about 12.21.12 and wondering what's going to happen. Writing in *Newsweek,* Lisa Miller notes, "The belief that the year 2012 will mark a global transformation is widespread."[11]

The date December 21, 2012 is already receiving more and more attention. It's hit cable news for sure, but it's especially proliferating on the Internet and in the blogosphere. Googling "2012" and "disaster" results in more than 2.5 million hits. Many people are buying into it—literally. Thousands are capitalizing on the hysteria, selling everything from survival kits and 2012 shelters to 2012 T-shirts. Several movies based on the 2012 theory are slated to come out in the next couple of years. And the video-sharing Web site YouTube hosts more than 65,000 clips informing and warning viewers about their fate in 2012.[12]

There are more 2012 Web sites than you could ever imagine. Here are ten examples:

survive2012.com

alignment2012.com

thisistheend.com

mayancalendar2012.org

howtosurvive2012.com

2012predictions.net

2012endofdays.org

apocalypse2012.com

december212012.com

2012theodyssey.com

Some of these Web sites provide an official 2012 countdown clock that will give you an up-to-the-second indicator of how long we have to wait for the end of the world to arrive!

Network news, cable channels, and major Internet outlets are all featuring programs and articles on the 2012 phenomenon. Here are just a few examples:

> History Channel: "Decoding the Past—Doomsday 2012: The End of Days"
>
> History Channel: "Decoding the Past—Mayan Doomsday Prophecy"
>
> History Channel: "The Lost Book of Nostradamus and 2012"
>
> AOL News: "Thousands Expect Apocalypse in 2012"[13]
>
> ABC News: "Will the World End in 2012? Thousands Worldwide Prepare for the Apocalypse, Expected in 2012"[14]
>
> *Fox & Friends:* "It's the End of the World: Mayan Calendar Ends in 2012"
>
> *Geraldo at Large* (Fox News): "Fact or Fiction: Will the World End in 2012?"
>
> *USA Today:* "Does Maya calendar predict 2012 apocalypse?"[15]
>
> *Los Angeles Times:* "Many gather to ponder end of Maya days"[16]

*New York Post:* "2012: The End Is Nigh!"[17]

*U.S. News & World Report:* "Apocalypse 2012: Are the Final Days Coming Soon? New Doomsdayers Adapt a Mayan Prediction"[18]

*Newsweek:* "2012: A Y2K for the New Age"[19]

Another barometer of the swelling interest in 2012 is the "Ask an Astrobiologist" section of NASA's Web site, where senior scientist David Morrison answers questions from the public. According to CNN, more than half of the inquiries on the "most popular" list were related to 2012.[20]

## iPhone Ultimate 2012

The familiar iPhone apps (applications) have even gone 2012. There's an iPhone app available for 99 cents that features an animated countdown to 12.21.12 called Ultimate 2012. The Ultimate 2012 app features "a task list maker, tip of the day called Drop of Knowledge, and an interactive Time Capsule. The task list has a subtle animated background, and a simple clean interface. The Drop of Knowledge gives you one piece of advice, or proverb, or survival tip to prepare for the big day. Aside from an info page, there's also a Time Capsule feature which lets you send messages to yourself which you cannot open until December 21, 2012."[21] There's even a short surprise video you can see when the final countdown hits 12.21.12.

## Rapping for 2012

The year 2012 is on the minds of a lot of people today. Even a couple of well-known rappers have embraced the 2012 deadline.

Germaine Williams, better known by his stage name Canibus, is a rapper. He is noted for his intricate and complex rhyme schemes and punch lines, as well as his sound technique and aptitude as a battle rapper. Canibus has released a CD called "Beyond 2012," which reveals and explains his interest in December 21, 2012.

Rapper Lil' Wayne, also known as Wheezy, after reading about Mayan prophecies while traveling around on his tour bus, is also convinced the world will end in a few years. According to *Starpulse,*

> The star has made the most of hours spent on the road, by learning about the ancient civilization. And he is sure recent events in world history prove the Mayans were right—and Armageddon will happen in 2012. He tells *Blender* magazine, "The world is about to end in 2012...'cause the Mayans made calendars, and they stop at 2012. I got encyclopedias on the bus. The world is about to end as we know it. You can see it already. A planet doesn't exist—there's no more Pluto. Planes are flying into buildings—and not just the Twin Towers. Mosquitos bite you and you die. And a black man and a woman are running for president."[22]

Girl Talk, a singing group led by Gregg Gillis, is taking things to the next level: post-apocalyptic. The group's farewell show is scheduled for December 21, 2012. Gillis says, "I want this to end when I'm on top. So I'm planning my final show on December 21, 2012. It's when the Mayan calendar ends. It's the day when solids become liquids and liquids become plasmas. So I'm building up to that—we've got four years."[23]

The fascination with 2012 is showing up everywhere. Expect more and more popular entertainers to jump on the 2012 bandwagon as the day draws near.

## Going Dutch

The 2012 fever is catching on in many places in the world, but the Dutch seem to be taking it much more seriously than many others. Fox News carried this report from the third-largest newspaper in the Netherlands:

> The world will end in 2012—or so say thousands in the Netherlands preparing for the apocalypse in four years, the Dutch-language newspaper *de Volkskrant* reported Tuesday. The paper spoke to those who believe the 2012 date signals the impending end of civilization and are stocking up on emergency supplies, equipment and life rafts in case of flooding, United Press International reported.
>
> While theories vary as to why 2012, in particular, is believed by some to represent the world's end, most say it is the end of the Mayan calendar. Some are optimistic about the apocalypse, saying they no longer want to live in the modern world.
>
> "You know, maybe it's really not that bad that the Netherlands will be destroyed," Petra Faile told *de Volkskrant*. "I don't like it here anymore. Take immigration, for example. They keep letting people in. And then we have to build more houses, which makes the Netherlands even heavier. The country will sink even lower, which will make the flooding worse." [24]

What's happening in the Netherlands may begin to gain traction in other parts of the world as 2012 approaches. Expect a growing survivalist movement and in some circles even a panic that will make the Y2K panic pale in comparison—especially if there are more global catastrophes during the next couple of years.

## *2012*—the Movie

It's no surprise that Hollywood is cashing in on the 2012 frenzy. Roland Emmerich's $200 million blockbuster, *2012*, released by Sony Pictures, is an apocalyptic tale of death, destruction, scorched earth, and all-out carnage of biblical proportions. The stunning preview shows the oceans washing over the Himalayas as a lone monk rings a huge gong in a futile attempt to warn people of what's coming. The final scene of the trailer shows a stunning image of the U.S.S. John F. Kennedy caught in a tsunami washing over Washington, D.C. and the White House.

It's reported that a third X-Files movie could be based around the emerging 2012 frenzy. Another movie, titled *2012: The War for Souls,* is a Michael Bay production based on *Communion* author Whitley Strieber's book of the same name. Michael Bay produced the movie *Transformers.* By the time 12.21.12 rolls around, there's no telling how many movies will give their version of the end of the world. As the movies about 2012 and the end of days hit the big screen, we can expect the countdown to 2012 to attract more attention.

## Why Another 2012 Book?

There's certainly no shortage of books and media exposure concerning the Mayan calendar and 2012. Books about 2012 are myriad and are flying off the shelves. When I entered "2012 prophecy" into an Amazon.com search, 187 results appeared. When I Googled "2012" there was a huge multitude of hits. New books are appearing on the Internet and in bookstores almost every month from publishers as large as HarperOne and as small as Bear & Company, a New Age publisher in Rochester, Vermont.[25]

Expect even more to come as the 2012 deadline draws near. There are titles like…

> *Apocalypse 2012: An Investigation into Civilization's End*
>
> *The Complete Idiot's Guide to 2012*
>
> *How to Survive 2012*
>
> *Maya Cosmogenesis 2012*
>
> *The Mystery of 2012: Predictions, Prophecies & Possibilities*
>
> *Fractal Time: The Secret of 2012 and a New World Age*
>
> *World Cataclysm in 2012*
>
> *How to Survive 2012*
>
> *The Maya End Times: Maya Prophecies for 2012*

So, why another book? What could I possibly say that has not already been said? Perhaps the best way to answer this question is to point to the title of the book. As the title suggests, my focus is to examine the 2012 phenomenon from a biblical perspective, primarily from the vantage point of end-time Bible prophecy. I believe the entire 2012 phenomenon is the eschatology of the New Age movement. It's their view of how this world will end or how a new age of human consciousness will begin.

While many other 2012 books mention the Bible or Bible codes, they don't look at 2012 through the lens of Scripture; rather, they look at Scripture through the lens of 2012. They pick and choose selected verses from the Bible, especially from the book of Revelation, to support their vision of what the future holds. By contrast, *2012, the Bible, and the End of the World* is unique. This book is written with one purpose in mind: to examine and expose the 2012 deadline in light of Bible prophecy and present what the Bible reveals about the end of the age.

## Final Answers

So, it's clear that December 21, 2012 is bearing down on planet earth and that a growing number of people are asking serious questions and are even making preparations. That much we know for sure. But what's it all about? What's the furor? Is there any truth to the 2012 doomsday theory? People everywhere are asking alarming questions:

- Are we in a race against time?
- Are natural disasters, plagues, and war signs of the times?
- Could December 21, 2012 be doomsday—the global tipping point?
- Why do so many believe it is?
- Are ancient prophecies being fulfilled today?
- Did Nostradamus point to 2012 as the end of days?
- Could Jesus return in 2012?
- Does the Bible say anything about 2012?
- Could this be Armageddon?
- Is there any hope for the future?

## Beyond the Headlights

Have you ever driven on a strange, dark road in a blinding rainstorm? The entire way, you wish you could see beyond the edge of the headlights. If only you could intuitively know what's out there or predict what you'll find at the next bend in the road! You long to see ahead so you can make sure you avert disaster.

Can someone see what's ahead by intuition or a special gift?

Can a prophet know the future because the path of our lives is part of a larger drama scripted ahead of time? Can we know where we are in that pattern of events foretold by sages and prophets, or from the ancient prophecies written in Scripture, or seen in apocalyptic visions of the future? That is what we'll explore in this book.

In the uncertain storm of the days in which we live, all of us yearn to see beyond the headlights. But can we?

2

# AN ANCIENT
# DOOMSDAY CLOCK?

"We are a people of destiny. Destined to be the masters
of time. Destined to be nearest to the gods."

MEL GIBSON (*APOCALYPTO*)

igns are mushrooming that we are living in a spiritually
prophetic age. Television documentaries, Web sites, books,
and YouTube videos depict volcanoes, floods, and category-5 hurricanes inundating the earth. Words such as *Armageddon, apocalypse,*
and *end of the world* are appearing in popular culture with ever
increasing regularity.

Modern man is asking questions about the future as never
before. They are solemn and searching questions. The rapidly
increasing tempo of life, combined with today's natural disasters, wars and rumors of wars, terrorism, and mounting financial
uncertainty, has given the entire world a sense of impending crisis.
The world appears to be running in a lemming-like rush toward
the day of reckoning.

Many have deep-seated questions about our times and are frantically searching for answers wherever they can find them. Intellectuals are looking to lost civilizations such as the Mayans; the uncertain predictions of Nostradamus, Mother Shipton, and Edgar Cayce; and the ancient Sibylline Oracles to satisfy a need for truth. Native American cultures such as the Hopi tribe of Arizona, Cherokee Indians of Oklahoma, and the Q'ero Indians of Peru are cited in support of a coming doomsday on or near 2012. Some have even dug up some of the psychic prophecies of old Merlin the magician to discover what he said about the end of the world. *I Ching,* the Chinese Book of Changes, which dates back almost 3000 years, is being consulted for its predictions about the end of days. The ancient prophecies of Revelation and Bible codes are once again being deciphered. But in this search for answers, many believe that the Mayans are the key. All these other sources are being checked out to corroborate what the Mayans said. According to 2012ologists, "The Mayan code is the master code. It's the galactic code."[1] And, according to the Mayan calendar, we are in the end times. The destruction of the current age is well under way.

Daniel Pinchbeck, a noted 2012 researcher, says,

> Our civilization is on a path of ever-increasing acceleration, but what are we rushing toward? Anxieties are multiplying. The environment is disintegrating. The heat is rising as the ozone layer thins. Jihad faces off against McWorld in senseless wars and televised atrocities. Populations are displaced as cities beneath toxic flood tides. Rogue nations stockpile nuclear arsenals...Military analysts prepare for resource wars fought over water and grain; indigenous prophecies point to an imminent polar reversal that will wipe our hard drives clean...According to

the sacred calendar of the Mayan and Toltec civilizations of Mesoamerica, this date signifies the end of a "Great Cycle" of more than five thousand years, and the conclusion of one world age and the beginning of the next.[2]

Gregg Braden, a 2012 researcher, asks and answers the all-important question many are posing: "Does the ancient Mayan calendar hold the secret to an epic event that will occur within our lifetimes? If so, does that event hold the key to our future, and perhaps even our very survival? A growing body of evidence suggests that the answer to these important questions is, Yes."[3]

According to meticulous Mayan calculations, the world as we know it is about to reach its expiration date. Interestingly, the ancient Aztec calendar corroborates the Mayan end date, also pointing to the end of the present cycle on December 21, 2012.[4]

Where did these predictions come from? What are they based on? What do they predict will happen? Are they reliable? And maybe most importantly, do these predictions have any relation to alarming events taking place in our world today?

Before we answer those questions, we need to find out more about the Maya. Just who were these ancient masters of time? Who were the mysterious Mayan timekeepers?

## Medieval Masters of Mesoamerica

The origin of the Mayans is shrouded in mystery. Some maintain that the Mayan lineage stretches back as far as 2000 years. No one knows for sure, but there are some things we do know. The Maya were not alone in ancient Mesoamerica. Several important neighbors shared the region. The Toltecs, who lived about 500 miles to the west in Central Mexico, spoke a different language but shared many of the Mayan beliefs about time, nature, and cosmology. The Toltec were a late arrival on the scene, emerging to power in about A.D. 900. The Olmec, another people group, were the first ones in the region to establish a major civilization. Their cultural influence peaked between 1500 and 600 B.C. Other Mayan neighbors were the Zapotec and Aztec.

The Mayans occupied eastern Mesoamerica, which today is the Yucatan Peninsula in Mexico, extending down into modern Guatemala, Honduras, and Belize. Mayan cities were large population centers. Tikal, a Mayan city in what is now Guatemala, had a population of about 50,000, had more than 3000 buildings, and covered an area of six square miles.[5]

| Archaeological Periods of Mayan History | |
|---|---|
| 1500 B.C.–200 B.C. | Pre-Classic period |
| 200 B.C.–A.D. 900 | Classical period |
| A.D. 900–1500 | Post-Classic period |

Mayan war monuments attest to the Mayans' ferocity in battle. "Kings did not plan wars and send young men to battle. They led the battles themselves, and if they lost, they were sacrificed so the people could continue."[6]

## The Vanishing

Mayan civilization enjoyed a peak population of five to fourteen million in about A.D. 800, yet only 100 years later they had diminished by 80-90 percent. Just like their origin, their sudden vanishing act is still veiled in mystery. What emptied their thriving cities and brought an end to their culture so suddenly? Theories abound: social/political upheaval, environmental breakdown (resulting in famine), or even sudden climate change.[7] Others point to some deadly plague. Yet the absence of vast gravesites or other telling signs of sudden, large-scale deaths argues against this idea.[8] The most accepted theory today is some kind of environmental collapse and resulting famine from overfarming, deforestation, and depleted soils.[9] While no one can be certain, a fatal combination of several causes makes the most sense. Nevertheless, wherever they came from and whatever happened to them, we know one main thing about the Maya: They were sky-watching timekeepers.

## Lords of Time

The Maya weren't just interested in time, they were obsessed with it. They were galactic masters. The Mayan calendar keepers painstakingly charted the cycles of the moon, the sun, and Venus. Their uncanny accuracy was not duplicated until modern times. As Lawrence Joseph notes, "Without telescopes or any other apparatus, Mayan astronomers calculated the length of the lunar month to be 29.53020 days, within 34 seconds of what we now know to its actual length of 29.53059 days. Overall, the 2000-year-old Mayan calendar is believed by many to be more accurate than the 500-year-old Gregorian calendar we use today."[10] Their solar year was estimated to be 365.2450 days minus an error of .0002. Our modern calendar calculates it as 365.2425 plus an error of .0003.[11] And the Mayan astronomers did all of this without the help of telescopes, computers, or calculators.

The Maya didn't keep track of time for just a few years, or even a few decades. They kept track of time for centuries, even millennia, up to 26,000 years. "For the Maya, time was holy. It had its own set of qualities that reflected in events. Time formed history, not the other way around…Time was not a succession of days; it was the enactment of a cosmic plan. The calendars contained the map of this plan"[12] The Mayan time codes are very elaborate and precise.

Like most premodern cultures, the Maya viewed history not as the linear passage of time but as a series of cycles that repeated over and over again. For them, it was all about numbers and cycles. Their calendars meticulously measured cycles.

## You Think Your Calendar Is Crowded

The Mayan obsession with time can be seen in the fact that they developed approximately 20 different calendars. While all of them are fascinating, the Maya relied upon three main time-tracking calendars—three calendars that are most relevant to the 2012 date. The solar calendar, known as the *Haab'*, or Vague Year, was based on the celestial cycle. It contained 365 days split into 18 months of 20 days each with one five-day period or "month" left over, which was considered very unlucky. The calendar was comprised of 20-day months because the Maya considered the number 20 to be sacred since each person has 20 digits.

The second calendar, called the *Tzolk'in,* was the ceremonial or sacred calendar and related to Venus' cycle. It contained 260 days known as the "sacred cycle." It is believed to be based on the nine-month period of human gestation. It has been referred to as the "Ritual Almanac and is regarded as the oldest and most widely used calendar in Mesoamerica."[13]

The third Mayan measure of time is known as the Long Count calendar. It was used to document the "world age cycles" that repeat over and over. This calendar was divided into five units that extend forward and backward from the mythical creation of the Maya, which they believed was August 11, 3114 B.C. That date is represented on the Mayan Long Count calendar as 0.0.0.0.1 (Day One). The fifth cycle is supposed to end on December 21, 2012 or 13.0.0.0.0 (Day Last). The day after will be 0.0.0.0.1 (but many don't believe that day will come). According to the Maya, all five great cycles are supposed to end in destruction. The year 2012 is the year that the fifth great cycle is supposed to end. This is the genesis of the belief that the end of days is 2012.

| Mayan Time on the Long Count Calendar |
|:---:|
| 1 baktun=144,000 days |
| 13 baktuns=1 great cycle (5125 years) |
| 5 great cycles=1 precessional cycle (25,625 years) |

A precessional cycle is the amount of time it takes for the earth to complete one full "wobble." We all know that the earth turns on its axis, but what some people do not know is that as the earth rotates, it wobbles very slightly. This wobble creates a small circle in the sky called the "precession." The earth wobbles one degree every 72 years. It takes approximately 25,800 years to complete one full precession called the "precession of the equinox." [14] To make it easier to remember, this number is often rounded to 26,000 years. This is about the same time as one grand cycle of the Mayan timekeeping system. Again, the Maya figured all this out without telescopes or computers. Their time system was so precise it has "not slipped one day in over twenty-five centuries." [15]

The 2012 date marks both the end of the fifth cycle and the end of a precessional cycle. It coincides with the "galactic alignment" of the sun and the earth with the "galactic equator" that bisects the black hole at the center of the Milky Way.

## The Mayan Apocalypse Comes of Age

The rare alignment in 2012 occurs only once every 26,000 years, as does the time it takes for the earth to complete one wobble around its axis. On December 21, 2012, the winter solstice for the northern hemisphere, the sun and earth will line up with the galactic center of the Milky Way. Because recorded history goes back only about 6000 years, we have no idea what happened the last time the solstice sun and earth lined up with the center of the Milky Way galaxy. We now live in the uncharted waters of the final great cycle.

We will cross the threshold of the Milky Way's equator in 2012. When that happens, we will begin a new 5125-year world age and also a new 26,000 year precessional cycle. Benjamin Anastas, a novelist and essayist, notes, "All the current hoopla is due to the mathematical fact that the current world-age cycle on the long count, which began in August 3114 B.C., is about to reach its end, 5126 years later, on a date given in scholarly notation as 13.0.0.0.0—which falls, not quite exactly, on Dec. 21, 2012. Enter the apocalypse…"[16]

Mayan cosmology predicts five cycles, each lasting 5125 years. Four have passed, each allegedly ending in destruction. The fifth cycle is set to end on December 21, 2012. Is this doomsday? "To know what conditions the 2012 calendar end date may have in store, it's important to bear in mind that 2012 marks the completion of not only one, but two nested cycles of time. The 5,125 year great cycle for world cycle that ends then is part of the larger 26,000-year precessional cycle that's also coming to a close at the same time."[17]

We'll complete both cycles simultaneously. They will converge in 2012. These two cycles share the same end date.

This alignment won't occur again for another 26,000 years. The big question is, What does it mean?

## The Jungle Book

Although the ancient Maya had a highly developed writing system and maintained meticulous records of key religious and historical events, almost none of their original writings are extant. These valuable documents were lost and destroyed when the Spanish conquistadors invaded Mesoamerica in the 1500s. Only three of these books and a fragment of a fourth are known to have survived the fires of conquest. They are known as the Dresden Codex, the Madrid Codex, the Paris Codex, and the Grolier Codex. The most elaborate, beautiful, complete, and best made of the Mayan codices is the Dresden Codex, which is best described as an eleventh-century Mayan picture book. It is 74 pages long, was made of a material from fig tree bark, and stretches to nearly 20 feet in length. Covered with paintings, including figures of the Mayan gods, the book is a Mayan hieroglyphic text that provides invaluable information about Mayan culture.

The history of the Dresden Codex is shrouded in mystery. A common theory is that it was taken from the Mayan temple and observatory at Chichen Itza by the Spanish conqueror Hernando Cortez and delivered to Emperor Charles V in about 1520. The Dresden Codex, known officially as *Codex Dresdensis,* derives its name from the place where it resides today—the Royal Library in Dresden, Germany. The book was purchased in 1739 from a collection in Vienna by the director of the Royal Library of Dresden, who gave it to the library in 1744. How the codex made its way to Austria is anyone's guess, but the most likely conjecture is that it was sent there by the king of Spain, who for a time was also the king of Austria.

The Dresden Codex is often considered to be a treatise on astronomy. It contains numerous astronomical calculations and eclipse-prediction tables. It focuses specifically on "Venus and the cycles of Venus that were used to predict the outcomes of war."[18] Due to its astronomical and predictive nature, the codex is consulted today by many to discover important clues about the end of the world and any relation it has to the 2012 end date. I watched a special on the History Channel about 2012 that claimed that the final page of the Dresden Codex predicts worldwide destruction by flood. But this appears to be less certain than the History Channel stated. Apparently the codex does contain a page about a great flood, often called the "flood page," which could be a prophecy of a massive flood or could refer to some past event, such as the biblical flood event, or even the Mayan rainy season. Others, however, maintain that the Mayan calendars say that this age will be destroyed by fire.[19] There is certainly no consensus about how the end will come, but the discovery of this codex was an important first step in understanding more about Mayan culture, language, and obsession with the heavens.

## A Star Is Born

The Milky Way was a major component in Mayan mythology. The Maya believed the center of the galaxy was the "womb of the world," the place where all stars were born. What's amazing is that modern science has discovered that there is a black hole at the center of the galaxy where all the stars in the Milky Way were born. An ancient Mayan symbol portrays the center of the Milky Way "as a whirling disc, much as we might draw a black hole."[20]

"In the absence of high-speed computers and complex software, they calculated the movement of the earth and our entire solar system as it relates to the core of our own Milky Way galaxy."[21] How does this relate to December 21, 2012? On that day the sun will block or eclipse the center of the galaxy, interrupting emissions or energy flow from the galactic center to the earth. What will happen when we enter the alignment zone? Or should we call it the "twilight zone"? Nobody knows for sure, but there's no shortage of doomsday theories.

## The Stones Cry Out

The Mayan obsession with time and astronomy is evident in their stunning architecture. Entire cities and buildings, including pyramids and temples, were laid out to align with astronomical events and reflect the cosmos. Even private homes were carefully aligned. The four corners of every house were aligned with the four cardinal directions (north, south, east, and west). Windows were carefully placed to make certain the sun shined on certain objects at certain times.

Synthia Andrews and Colin Andrews observe,

> The Mayan encrypted the pyramids they built with information from their calendars. Information is reflected in the mathematics of the design and the number of stairs, angles, segments; all had relationship to the length of the Mayan ages, the solar year, specific dates, and more. In addition to being observatories, these are teaching devices, universities in stone—books to withstand the march of time.[22]

Few people probably realize that the Mayan pyramids are older than the ones in Egypt. To put the Mayan pyramids in historical perspective, the pyramid in Cuicuilco, Mexico was constructed in 2750 B.C., about the same time that Stonehenge was built in England. The Great Pyramid in Egypt was built about 200 years later, in 2560 B.C.[23] It is fascinating that all these mysterious stone structures were built around the same time in places that were so distant from one another.

## Building Codes

The Mayan pyramids are amazing structures and were startling cosmograms (symbols of the cosmos) in stone. Their buildings and cities are mirrors of the Mayan cosmos. Here's one astounding example:

> Chichen Itza is probably the most visited and best known site in the Yucatan. One can visit the Great Ballcourt, the Pyramid of Kukulcan, the Hall of Atlantean Columns, the Caracol observatory, and the Sacred Wall (the cenote). But the city's biggest attraction is an amazing astronomical event that occurs every spring equinox. On this day, March 21, thousands of visitors pack in around the Pyramid of Kukulcan and prepare to watch the shadow-play caused by the late afternoon sun. Around 4:00 P.M., the rays of the sun cast a shadow that looks like an undulating snake onto the side of the north stairway. A serpent's head carved in stone at the base of the stairway completes the picture of an upside-down serpent—a deity-serpent descending from the sky—that is quite common in Mesoamerican art. One can imagine that the snake's tail, or rattle points through the roof of the little room on top of the pyramid. Visitors go away from this experience

amazed at the sophisticated and ingenious people who
could build a mythological story into their monumental
architecture.[24]

Kukulkan, also known as Quetzalcoatl, was the feathered serpent or plumed god. The Pyramid of Kukulkan, which is also
called El Castillo, has a large serpent's head at its base. When the
shadow of the serpent slithers down and reaches the bottom of
the pyramid, "it unites with the sculpted head of Kukulkan."[25]
For the Maya, this symbolizes the return of Kukulkan or Quetzalcoatl. To this day, at the spring solstice, 50,000 people gather
at Chichen Itza to witness this event.

The Toltec people, who lived in central and northern Mexico,
used the same basic calendars as the Maya—a 260-day sacred
calendar and a 365-day calendar. Every day on both calendars
was given a name. When the Toltecs migrated to Maya country in the Yucatan Peninsula, they merged their cosmology with
the Mayan system and encoded it in the Pyramid of Kukulkan
at Chichen Itza. "The pyramid has 91 steps on each of its four
sides, totaling 364, plus the top step: 365 altogether. This is a clear
sign of calendrical meaning."[26] The terraces of the pyramid are
divided into 18 segments, which reflect the number of months
in the Mayan *Haab'* calendar.[27] The precision of these structures
is staggering, even in the age of supercomputers.

## Take Me Out to the Ball Game

Like people everywhere, the Maya loved their sports, especially one involving a ball and a goal. Thirteen ball courts have
been discovered in the city of Chichen Itza alone, including the
largest one discovered so far, the Great Ballcourt. The Mayan ball

game was pretty simple. It included the court, players, a ball, a goal (in the shape of a ring), a center marker, and game equipment.[28] But what the game symbolized was anything but simple. The game and the layout of the ball court carried cosmic significance. And there was one pretty tough rule: If you lost, you paid the ultimate sacrifice.

John Major Jenkins provides this description of the Maya ball game and its symbolic meaning:

> The Great Ballcourt at Chichen Itza, located a short distance northwest of the Pyramid of Kukulcan, was oriented to the Milky Way on the June solstice in the era A.D. 865. At midnight on every June solstice during this era, the long axis of the ballcourt point to where the Milky Way touched the horizon. The body of the Milky Way arched through the sky, mirroring the ballcourt itself, and the dark-rift of the Milky Way would have been observed overhead. In other words, it appears the designers of the Chichen's ballcourt intended to mirror the dark-rift in the Milky Way with the orientation of the ceremonial ballcourt...In the relationship between the Milky Way and the Great Ballcourt just described, the dark-rift is the "central hole" of the Milky Way ballcourt; in other words, it is the cosmic goalring. Its cosmological meaning include a center and navel of the sky, a portal to other dimensions, and a place of rebirth. This is where the Solar deity—the big game-ball—will be reborn at the end of the current era.[29]

What does all this mean for 2012? Simply stated, Jenkins' in-depth analysis of the galactic cosmology at Chichen Itza leads him to the conclusion that the final victory in the "ball game" portrays the end of the great cycle on 13.0.0.0.0—end date December 21, 2012!

## How Did They Know All This?

Think about what the Mayans knew. With the naked eye, they calculated the length of a solar day with a precision that rivals our modern knowledge; their "calendar priests" charted a 26,000-year astronomical cycle, known as the precession of the equinoxes; they understood that the center of our galaxy is where the stars in this galaxy were born; and they were able to construct elaborate, precise, massive stone structures that reflected uncanny insight into the deepest inner workings of our galaxy. The question I was left asking is, Where did they learn all this? As I researched these ancient timekeepers, I often wondered, *How did they attain this advanced level of knowledge and understanding?* There's a lot of speculation as to the answer.

Some point to UFOs as the answer. Visitors from the skies are viewed as the only possible source for this kind of complex knowledge. Others conjecture that this highly developed insight was passed to the ancient Egyptians, Mayans, and other sophisticated civilizations in the ancient world by the survivors of the mystical Atlantis. Another possibility, not mentioned by 2012ologists, is that they learned it from their gods, which were not gods at all, but demonic spirits that could have communicated this sophisticated knowledge to them. Much of the barbaric, bloodthirsty "worship" of the Mayans, including human sacrifices, can be accounted for if we recognize that it was demonically motivated by the real power behind their gods of stone.[30] It makes sense to me that the same spirits that inspired their religion would have communicated to them the hidden secrets of the cosmos.

Nevertheless, whatever the source of their incredible knowledge, these ancient calendar priests were on a galactic treasure hunt, searching for the master key to unlock the deepest mysteries of time, history, and the future, which was the holy grail of these ancient timekeepers.

## The Mayan Alarm Clock

It wasn't until 1950, after decades of painstaking research, that Mayan scholars were able to correlate the Mayan calendar with our modern calendar. It was then that December 21, 2012 was determined to be the end date of the world.[31]

Centuries ago, long before the invention of even the simplest telescope, the Maya were aware of the galactic alignment of the sun with the center of the Milky Way in 2012, and "just like an alarm clock they set their calendar to coincide with the occasion."[32] It's clear that the Mayan alarm clock is about to go off. The galactic alignment timer is set to go off on 12.21.12.

Will 2012 be the final winter? When the sun and earth move into direct alignment with the center of the Milky Way galaxy, what will happen? A growing number of people are convinced that *something* is going to happen—something big.

The question is, What?

# Apocalypse Now?

## Predictions, Prophecies, and Possibilities

"December 21, 2012: When Earth aligns with the exact center of the galaxy, the Mayan calendar ends. Homo sapiens will...die."

WHITLEY STRIEBER (*2012: THE WAR FOR SOULS*)

"How would the governments of our planet prepare six billion people for the end of the world?...They wouldn't."

*2012* (MOVIE TRAILER)

The headline was seen all over the world. The first news item that flashed across the Internet on July 6, 2008 was an article titled "Thousands Expect Apocalypse in 2012." The article was excerpted from an ABC News investigation on the global rise in "doomsday cults." The opening sentence of the article said it all: "Survival groups around the world are gearing up and counting down to a mysterious date that has been anticipated for thousands of years: December 21, 2012."[1]

The same article says, "From across the United States, Canada and throughout Europe, apocalyptic sects and individuals say that is the day [December 21, 2012] that the world as we know it will end." Since then, the matter of 2012 has erupted on the scene. People everywhere are asking questions about this fast-approaching end date.

## Apocalypse New

The apocalypse has man firmly held in its collective grip. Movies and television shows regularly spew out the message of cataclysm and world destruction by massive tidal waves, earthquakes, volcanoes, alien attacks, comets, asteroids, or a nuclear holocaust. The dreaded "end of the world" has almost been reduced to a cultural cliché.

There's what we might call a growing "doom boom" in the world. Pop culture has gone apocalyptic. Some have called it "apocalypse new" and questioned "why we can't wait for the end of the world."[2] When you stop and think about it, all kinds of apocalyptic visions surround us. In the summer of 1998 a blockbuster movie about an asteroid the size of Texas on a collision course with earth was titled *Armageddon*. McDonald's joined forces with the movie company and offered their drinks and French fries in *Armageddon* cups and boxes. As I saw the commercials for this movie and drank my Coke at McDonald's out of a cup with the word *Armageddon* emblazoned on it, I couldn't help but wonder if the movie producer had any idea what the word *Armageddon* means. I also wondered how many of the millions of moviegoers had a clue about the true meaning of Armageddon.

The cinema blockbuster *I Am Legend*, starring Will Smith, features New York City after a genetically modified virus kills most humans and alters others into wild, vampire-like monsters. Cormac McCarthy's bestseller *The Road* is a postapocalyptic novel set in the ravaged landscape of postnuclear America. *The Day the Earth Stood Still* chronicles an alien invasion and massive annihilation. *Knowing* is a cinematic apocalypse starring Nicolas Cage. It centers on a document containing a long series of numbers that symbolize every cataclysm of the past 50 years. The last few numbers hold all-important clues about catastrophes that have yet to occur. With life in the balance, it's up to Massachusetts Institute of Technology professor John Koestler (played by Cage) to decode the mysterious prophecy. The most gripping scene is the New York skyline wipeout. *Terminator Salvation* is set in 2018 America and features a cataclysm called Judgment Day, which takes place after *Terminator 3: Rise of the Machines.* Before all these newer versions of the postapocalypse there was the Mad Max trilogy, which pictures the dystopia that remains after a worldwide oil shortage led to nuclear war.

On top of all this, there's *2012,* the movie to end all movies. Am I missing something, or is there some growing corporate vision that the world is getting near "closing time"?

## 2012 Watch

When our rendezvous with 2012 arrives, what on earth will happen? The last time a similar alignment of planets and stars occurred was before recorded history, so there is all kinds of speculation about what could happen. There are many predictions about what to expect on 12.21.12. The *New York Post* has even put a humorous twist on 2012:

> The end of the world is nearly upon us, but there's a silver lining: At least you know when your 401(k) will finally hit bottom. Mark Dec. 21, 2012 on your calendar. That's the exact day that lots of normally sane people believe some disaster will befall our planet—and not the kind of

annoying everyday disaster like your cable going out or
Ethan Hawke writing another novel. We're talking Biblical
proportions—the end of life on Earth as we know it.[3]

But what are 2012 enthusiasts saying? The possibilities are
far-ranging: from peace to polar shift, from annihilation to awakening, from terror to transformation. In the movie *2012* the
world faces unprecedented cataclysm in the form of volcanic
eruptions, typhoons, and overwhelming floods. While there are
many divergent opinions about what will happen in 2012, there
are six main forecasts about what to expect. Let's briefly consider each one.

## Polar Opposites

The majority view among 2012 followers seems to be that
December 2012 will usher in the apocalypse. They believe that
earth's expiration date is clearly marked out for everyone to see.
Civilization as we know it will cease to exist, with 90 percent loss
of life for all species, including man. There are all kinds of ideas
about what will happen and what will cause the cataclysm. One
of the leading 2012 doomsday theorists is Patrick Geryl. ABC
News provides this information about Geryl:

> Two years ago, Patrick Geryl, then 51, quit his job as a
> laboratory worker for a French oil company. He'd saved
> up just enough money to last him until December 2012.
> After that, he thought, he wouldn't need it anyway. Instead,
> Geryl, a soft-spoken man who had studied chemistry in
> his younger years, started preparing for the apocalypse.
> He founded a "survival group" for likeminded men and
> women, aimed at living through the catastrophe he knew
> was coming.

He started gathering materials necessary to survive—water purifiers, wheelbarrows (with spare tires), dust masks and vegetable seeds. His list of survival goods runs 11 pages long. "You have to understand, there will be nothing, nothing left," Geryl told ABC News from his home in Antwerp, Belgium. "We will have to start an entire civilization from scratch."[4]

The ABC News interview with Geryl ended when he was asked what would happen if December 2012 were to come and go without the earthquakes and tsunamis he anticipates. In response to that question, Geryl fell silent, then said, "I don't really contemplate that possibility. [My predictions] are so spectacular, they can't possibly be wrong."

According to Geryl's Web site, howtosurvive2012.com, he is now devoting his time to forming a survival group. He believes that 2012 will usher in colossal disasters that will kill billions of people. His basic thesis is that December 2012 will bring a reversal of the magnetic poles of the sun, resulting in the release of solar flares that "lash out into the solar system," causing the earth's magnetic poles to reverse, that is, the north pole becomes south and the south pole become north. This geomagnetic reversal could cause devastation or possibly no real, noticeable change. But Geryl theorizes that this same kind of pole shift is what destroyed ancient Atlantis on July 27, 9792 B.C., and that a few priests who survived that disaster passed their knowledge on to warn mankind of the next great cataclysm. The knowledge was supposedly stored in the labyrinth (Circle of Gold) in Egypt and was later transmitted to future generations, including the Maya.

There are a couple of obvious problems with Geryl's view. First, he presupposes that ancient Atlantis existed, a matter that is far from certain. Second, he assumes that a similar polar shift ended civilization on July 27, 9792 B.C. Neither of those facts can be proven conclusively, especially the very specific date he gives for Atlantis' disappearance. Also, how did this information get from Egypt to Mesoamerica?[5]

Still, as you can imagine, Geryl maintains that the coming pole shift will wreak havoc. On the back cover of his book *How to Survive 2012*, he writes, "The Earth's outer crust is thrown into chaos, with planet-wide earthquakes, volcanoes and tidal waves. Civilization as we know it will end. Billions of casualties will occur worldwide; very few humans will survive." Geryl solemnly concludes, "This gigantic geological disaster will thoroughly destroy our civilization."[6]

He, along with many others, follows this dire prediction with the terrible results of the solar pole shift.

1. A huge cloud of electromagnetic particles will be released into space, completely destroying all satellites around the earth.

2. Massive earthquakes and volcanic outbursts. (The glacial lake at Yellowstone National Park sits on top of the world's most dangerous supervolcano hot spot. When it blows, it will plunge the globe into a nuclear winter. The Yellowstone caldera is building up pressure and, like a ticking time bomb, is due to blow anytime. A rise in seismic and volcanic activity is expected in—you guessed it—2011-12.[7] Also, solar maximum energies expected at that time could precipitate an eruption of biblical proportions.)

3. Drastic climate change. The U.S. and Europe will enter a new ice age.

4. Tidal waves will destroy food supplies and con-
taminate water supplies.

5. Drilling installations will be torn apart, contami-
nating the oceans.

6. Harbors and ships will be completely devastated.
Transportation will cease.

7. Nuclear plants will be destroyed by shifting in the
earth's crust releasing radioactive contamination.

8. Health services will be unavailable.

9. All lines of communication will be severed.

10. Electromagnetic storms will make air travel
impossible.[8]

Pretty bleak, huh?

Geryl's end-of-days hypothesis is stunningly cataclysmic and complete. He believes that it was an earlier cycle of this same event, thousands of years ago, that brought about the demise of the dinosaurs. He concludes that "the story of the Swiss Family Robinson shipwrecked on a tropical island would be an absolute utopia compared to this destroyed and polluted world."[9] In another of his books, *The World Cataclysm in 2012,* Geryl states that in 2012 there will be "an enormous shift in the earth's crust. Virtually nobody will survive this, and at the same time all our acquired knowledge will disappear."[10] He hopes that the few who are prepared and survive will be able to reestablish civilization and repopulate human life on earth. Geryl's view is apocalypse gone wild. It's the end of days on steroids.

However, even more measured 2012ologists, such as Lawrence Joseph, point to 2012 as a time of widespread devastation. "Whether the birth agony of a New Age or simply the death throes of our current era, a disturbing confluence of scientific, religious, and historical trends indicates that an onslaught of disasters and revelations, man-made, natural, and quite possibly supernatural, will culminate tumultuously."[11]

## Solar Armageddon

Added to the dreaded pole shift hypothesis is the threat that 2012 will be a peak year for the sun's cycle, which will result in a dramatic increase in solar flares. To make it even more dire, NASA reports that 2012 will bring the most intense cycle of maximum sunspot activity since 1958. It's predicted that the sunspot surge in 2012 will be 30-50 percent stronger than what happened in 1958. No one knows what effect this will have, because there was very little satellite technology in 1958 to measure the upcoming situation against. Some say this dramatic influx of magnetic radiation could be catastrophic, causing major shifts in the jet stream and major ocean currents.[12] Compounding the situation is the fact that the planetary tidal force (the earth's gravitational pull on the sun) is also expected to peak in 2012.[13] There are predictions of wave after wave of Katrina-force storms slamming the U.S. coastline that could cause such devastation to infrastructure, oil supply, and loss of life that the world economy would collapse.

How worried should we be? While some weather changes, such as El Niño and La Niña, could certainly result from increased solar activity, gigantic flares have hit the earth before, and they didn't come even close to being extinction-level events. Supposedly, "solar activity can cause blackouts, as it did in Canada in 1989, but that's about the extent of it."[14]

The 2012 solar storm theory is not limited to 2012ologists. A new study from the National Academy of Sciences outlines grim possibilities on earth for a worst-case scenario solar storm. According to the report, the sun goes through an 11-year cycle, and in the active phase of this cycle can emit powerful solar magnetic storms that can fry electric transformers. Many experts are expecting a sunspot megacycle in 2012 that could produce a "Katrina from outer space." The menace of sun storms is very real. If the U.S. electric grid and satellites were to go down, the resulting devastation would be Katrina times ten. Everything from sewage systems to Wall Street banks would be affected, paralyzing the United States and other highly developed nations for months and maybe even years. According to a report from Fox News:

> The worst storms can knock out power grids by inducing currents that melt transformers. Modern power grids are so interconnected that a big space storm—the type expected to occur about once a century—could cause a cascade of failures that would sweep across the United States, cutting power to 130 million people or more in this country alone, the new report concludes...Impacts would be felt on interdependent infrastructures with, for example, potable water distribution affected within several hours; perishable foods and medications lost in 12-24 hours; immediate or eventual loss of heating/air conditioning, sewage disposal, phone service, transportation, fuel resupply and so on, the report states. Outages could take months to fix, the researchers say. Banks might close, and trade with other countries might halt.[15]

A humongous solar storm hit the United States in 1859 long before satellites and electricity were developed, yet it evidently shorted out telegraph wires in the United States and Europe. Sun storms have affected the United States in modern times. "In 1989, the sun unleashed a tempest that knocked out power to all of Quebec, Canada. A remarkable 2003 rampage included 10 major solar flares over a two-week period, knocking out two Earth-orbiting satellites and crippling an instrument aboard a Mars orbiter."[16]

Could a game-changing solar storm hit in 2012? The answer is that no one knows for sure. It could. But even the National Academy of Sciences admits that "widespread power outages would be a rare possibility."[17] But even if such outages occur at some point, this will not usher in the end of the world or some quantum leap in human consciousness. It would be a terrible disaster, but as far as I have been able to determine, no scientists connect this possibility with the notion of galactic alignment in 2012. Ian O'Neill concludes,

> So, regardless of prophecy, prediction or myth, there is no physical way to say that the Earth will be hit by *any* flare, let alone a big one in 2012. Even if a big flare did hit us, it will not be an extinction event. Yes, satellites may be damaged, causing secondary problems such as a GPS loss (which *might* disrupt air traffic control for example) or national power grids may be overwhelmed by auroral electrojets, but nothing more extreme than that.[18]

## Heads Up!

Another 2012 doomsday theory, commonly known as the Planet X hypothesis, theorizes that the earth is on a collision course, or will at least have a very close call, with the tenth planet of our solar system, known as Planet X. The official name of the planet is 2003UB313.[19] Some believe that ancient Sumerian astronomers identified the planet 5000 years ago and named it *Nibiru*. The *New York Post* describes the Nibiru hypothesis:

Adherents to this theory believe that there is a massive planet (nicknamed Nibiru) whose elliptical orbit will bring it into our solar system in 2012, causing calamity on Earth. The existence of a 10th planet or dwarf star lying on the edge of our solar system was first suggested by astronomers in the 19th and early 20th centuries, who observed irregularities in the orbits of Uranus and Neptune. They speculated the irregularity was due to gravitational pull by a giant object nearby. In 1983, a NASA satellite discovered a mystery object some 50 billion miles away. Doomsday theorists postulate that this object has been moving toward earth ever since and will come close enough in 2012 to wreak havoc with the sun and our planet's climate.[20]

According to Jacco van der Worp, the Planet X "flyby" will trigger a "cosmic slow motion train wreck" that will kill most of the earth's population and usher in "humanity's next golden Renaissance."[21]

The Web site 2012warning.com champions the Planet X speculation and describes what is expected to happen in 2012:

There is a planet that orbits our sun every 3600 years. This planet has been referred to as Planet X. It gets its name from being an elusive planet. The first real pictures of Planet X were photographed shortly after January 26, 1983, when NASA launched the Infrared Astronomical Satellite (IRAS). The astronomers calculated that Planet X was over 50 million miles away from us at that time. In 2004 Planet X was determined to be only 7 million miles away. It's moving closer. Confirmation of the tenth planet "Planet X" was photographed in Japan on February 28, 2008. Planet X exists, and it will be here by the end of 2012. *Planet X will appear as two suns in the sky to us, no later than 2011.*[22]

The Web site goes on to mention two Bible passages that it believes support this theory:

### Isaiah 13

They are coming from a far country, from the farthest horizons, the LORD and His instruments of indignation, to destroy the whole land...Therefore I will make the heavens tremble, and the earth will be shaken from its place (Isaiah 13:5,13).

### Revelation 6

I looked when He broke the sixth seal, and there was a great earthquake; and the sun became as black as sackcloth made of hair, and the whole moon became like blood; and the stars of the sky fell to the earth, as a fig tree casts its unripe figs when shaken by a great wind. The sky was split apart like a scroll when it is rolled up, and every mountain and island were moved out of their places. Then the kings of the earth and the great men and the commanders and the rich and the strong and every slave and free man hid themselves in the caves and among the rocks of the mountains; and they said to the mountains and to the rocks, "Fall on us and hide us from the presence of Him who sits on the throne, and from the wrath of the Lamb" (Revelation 6:12-16).

Neither of those Bible passages have anything to do with 2012 or Nibiru. Isaiah 13 looks to the final destruction of the city of Babylon, not the destruction of the world. Revelation 6:12-16 is God's direct judgment on the world in the end times for its sin, and there is no mention of any planet hitting the earth and no mention of any specific date. The Greek word translated "stars" is *asteres*. It is broad enough to include the smaller objects that plunge through space from time to time. According to Revelation 6, whatever happens will be significant enough that it will appear from man's perspective that the stars are falling. The best way to describe this is probably a massive meteor shower.[23] Clearly, whatever happens in Revelation 6:12-15 is not the mass extinction of humanity, because in the next chapter, Revelation 7, two great groups of people are described—144,000 witnesses and an innumerable host. That many people couldn't survive a collision between earth and Planet X.

In addition, I haven't been able to find a single credible scientist who gives any weight at all to the Planet X theory. This theory is best left to the domain of Sumerian myth.

## Transformation of Global Consciousness

As you can see, there are very different ideas about what 2012 will bring, yet all 2012 watchers agree that it will be a year of tremendous change—that it will be the defining moment of epochal, transcendent change. It's important to note that for many 2012 devotees, these various doomsday theories are not mutually exclusive. Polar shift, global warming, and Nibiru could come together to create a fatal combination.

Proponents of the 2012 theory agree that the Mayans believed the world would "end" in A.D. 2012, but they are divided on what that means. Is it literal or metaphorical? As we have seen, those who take the prediction literally envision this change as an impending doomsday, an epic disaster. Yet others are expecting a kinder, gentler time of transformation and a new beginning. For them, 2012 will bring the dawn of a new golden age, an age of awakening, a shift in the collective consciousness, a new plane of existence, or even a new step in human evolution akin to Stephen

J. Gould's theory of punctuated equilibrium. Those who adopt the metaphorical viewpoint anticipate a dramatic shift in world consciousness. For some who hold to the shift in consciousness theory, the process is not viewed as the result of a single cataclysmic event, but rather, as something that will evolve over a period of time beginning on or about 2012. At this point, 2012ology strongly intersects with the New Age movement. The shift that's expected in 2012 is described variously as

> "emotional and spiritual transformations"
>
> "the birth of our higher selves"[24]
>
> "an end-of-cycle reality check"
>
> "a pole shift in our collective psyche"[25]
>
> "the birth of a new species: 'homo spiritus'"[26]
>
> "a zone of alignment"[27]
>
> "the gateway to a new epoch of planetary development with a radically different kind of consciousness."[28]

This is the vocabulary of New Age thinking. You might be asking, "What exactly is the New Age movement?"

## New Age Mysticism

New Age thinking, which is rooted in the counterculture of the 1960s, encompasses a very broad scope of ideas and practices that emphasize what we might refer to as a kind of scientific mysticism. New Agers and their gurus are commonly associated with crystals, pyramids, channeling the voices of departed spirit guides, and cosmic convergences. They frequently hitch their ideological wagon to astronomy and astrology, as is the case with 2012. They reject biblical Christianity and deny the notion of a sinful human nature as a myth. Politically, they are often utopians. Author Ed Hindson summarizes the New Age movement well:

> New age thinking is a do-it-yourself religion with a smorgasbord of options: spiritism, witchcraft, channeling, transcendentalism, Oriental mysticism, and transtemporal psychology. Intellectually, it grows out of the belief that the world is now evolving spiritually, producing a great "planetary consciousness" that will eventually lead to a whole new order. New agers are calling for the total transformation of society along social and political lines— a transformation consistent with their own beliefs. They see mankind emerging into human consciousness and potential by declaring its own deification, leaving God "watching from a distance."[29]

New Age thinking carries an aura of getting in touch with nature and the beliefs and practices of traditional native cultures. A few of the leading 2012ologists claim to be shamans, or intermediaries between this world and the spirit world.

The New Age movement, which is part of the great paradigm shift of our times, is basically all about getting in touch with one's higher self and the emergence of a new planetary consciousness in human beings. Much of the revival of New Age thinking has been fueled by the teachings of Eckhart Tolle, who has been popularized with the help of Oprah Winfrey. Some of his bestselling books are titled *A New Earth: Awakening to Your Life's Purpose, Practicing the Power of Now, Oneness with All Life,* and *Guardians of Being.* The heading on his Web site reads, "Are you ready to be awakened?" With people like this behind it, it's clear that it's not a passing fad.

John Major Jenkins, a noted expert on Mesoamerican cosmology and 2012, reflects New Age mysticism. "My metaphorical interpretation is the Maya believed that around the year we call 2012, a large chapter in human history will be coming to an end. All the values and assumptions of the previous World Age will expire, and a new phase of human growth will commence."[30] He further observes,

> The ancient Maya understood something about the nature of the cosmos and the spiritual evolution of humanity that has gone unrecognized in our own worldview. The understanding involves our alignment with the center of the Galaxy, our cosmic center and source, and identifies A.D. 2012 as a time of tremendous transformation and opportunity for spiritual growth a transition from one World Age to another.[31]

Jenkins adds, "Around the year we call 2012 a large chapter in human history will be coming to an end. All the values and assumptions of the previous World Age will expire, and a new phase of human growth will commence."[32]

In his book *2012: The Return of Quetzalcoatl,* Daniel Pinchbeck advances the thesis that 2012 will bring a new state of human consciousness or "new intensity of awareness that will manifest itself as a different understanding, a transformed realization, of time and space and self."[33] Pinchbeck has traveled to numerous indigenous cultures exploring and incorporating their belief systems and practices. He advocates using psychedelic substances to enhance one's intellectual, spiritual, and psychological prowess and awareness.

Pinchbeck explains that for the Maya, the end of the great cycle "was associated with the return of the Mesoamerican deity Quetzalcoatl, 'Sovereign Plumed Serpent."[34] Pinchbeck doesn't believe in a literal advent of the Mayan god, but maintains that the legend of his return serves as an archetype that "points toward a shift in the nature of the psyche." So, his theory of 2012 is that it will bring about "the transformation of our consciousness," a "quantum jump into a new context" that will, in turn, "lead to the rapid creation, development, and dissemination of new institutions and social structures, corresponding to our new level of mind. From the limits of our current chaotic and uneasy circumstances, this process may well resemble and advance toward a harmonic, perhaps even utopian, situation on earth."[35] The year 2012, then, marks not a time of destruction, but rather a time of global purification and transformation. Not "the end of the world, but the end of a world, and the opening of a next."[36]

Daniel Pinchbeck chronicles what he has learned through his own New Age journeys: "Through my own shamanic journeys, I realized that modern culture was facing an initiatory crisis on a global scale. We have created a planet of 'kidults,' perpetual adolescents trapped by material desires, with no access to higher realms and little sense of purpose or moral responsibility."[37]

I would agree that many people in our world are absorbed with materialistic pursuits, but how will a galactic alignment or even a global crisis change that? The world has experienced horrible crises many times in the past. Sure, they can bring people closer together for a while and cause people to reflect in ways they haven't before, but it doesn't take long before man's inhumanity to man begins to surface again. Man cannot usher in his own utopia by some shift in consciousness. John Lennon sang about people living in peace, yet the Beatles could not even get along with each other. Almost half of the marriages in the United States fail. Many people don't even get along with their own families. How will an instantaneous quantum shift change the fallen nature of man? We should all do all we can to get along with one another, but tragically, man's sinful nature stands firmly in the way of any vision of utopia on earth by human means.

Hwee-Jong Jang, a business professor in South Korea, has written a book titled *The Gaia Project 2012: The Earth's Coming Great Changes.* The cover refers to the book as "A Guide to the Profound Transformation & Consciousness Shift." Jang claims that through revelation communicated to him through channeling, dreams, and energy readings he can explain countless mysteries and prepare people for the "Great Change" and "universal expansion of consciousness."[38] Consciousness will be raised and expanded on a global scale (whatever that means). At this point, much of the 2012 teaching gets pretty "out there." To me, it's *Twilight Zone* stuff. It's the same New Age mysticism recycled in a new package. Some are even claiming that the pace of evolution is accelerating and that humans are transforming into a new species. To give you some idea of the kind of rebirth themes about 2012 that are circulating, here are some of the chapter titles in the book *The Mystery of 2012*, which was written by leading authorities on the 2012 phenomenon.

"The Birthing of a New World"

"2012: Socially Responsible Business and Nonadversarial Politics"

"Wild Love Sets Us Free"

"An Awakening World"

"The Advent of the Post-Human Geo-Neuron"

"How the Snake Sheds Its Skin: A Tantric Path to Global Transformation"

"2012: Awakening to Greater Reality"

Experts on 2012 are calling people to get ready for this shift to make sure they can survive 2012. I agree that we should all love one another and seek for peace and harmony based on real truth.

This is a central teaching of Jesus and the Bible. But the notion that this will happen by man's efforts apart from God's help is sheer fantasy. The claim we will enter a new age of human consciousness merely because of a galactic alignment is untenable. Humanity's problems come from within, and external events cannot change human nature.

## End of Days, New Golden Age, or Both?

What are we to make of all this? Some are expecting A.D. 2012 to be a dramatic end, others are expecting a glorious new beginning or rebirth, and still others believe it will be both—an end and a new beginning, the prelude for global renewal. Lawrence Joseph argues for this "middle-case scenario":

> The Mayan calendar tells us what's ahead for the whole world. On 12/21/12 our Solar System, with the Sun at its center, will, as the Maya have for millennia maintained, eclipse the view from Earth of the center of the Milky Way. This happens only once every 26,000 years. Ancient Mayan astronomers considered this center spot to be the Milky Way's womb, a belief now supported by voluminous evidence that that's where the galaxy's stars are created. Astronomers now suspect that there is a black hole right at the center sucking up the matter, energy, and time that will serve as raw materials for the creation of future stars. In other words, whatever energy typically streams to Earth from the center of the Milky Way will indeed be disrupted on 12/21/12, at 11:11 pm Universal Time, for the first time in 26,000 years.[39]

Joseph then provides this analogy:

> The best analogy is the way that even a momentary

disruption of electrical power can cause the clocks on VCRs and microwaves to go from keeping perfect time to blinking on and off meaninglessly until they are reset by hand. Our being even briefly cut off from the emanations from the center of the galaxy will, the Maya believe, throw out of kilter vital mechanisms of our bodies and of the Earth.[40]

He then states what he believes will happen:

2012 is destined to be a year of unprecedented turmoil and upheaval. Whether the birth agony of a New Age or simply the death throes of our current era, a disturbing confluence of scientific, religious, and historical trends indicates that an onslaught of disasters and revelations, man-made, natural, and quite possibly supernatural, will culminate tumultuously…there is at least an even chance of some massive tragedy and/or great awakening occurring or commencing in that year. The question ultimately is not if but when…[41]

James O'Dea views 2012 as a kind of judgment for man's transgressions:

This is one aspect of the meaning of 2012: it's humanity's pay date—the due date when our debt will be maxed, and no further credit from a depleted and overtaxed Nature will be extended to us. It is also the time when Nature's wake-up call, already sounding loudly, will reverberate through the psyche of humanity as a collective experience, as a shared frequency or resonance.[42]

For O'Dea, 2012 will be a time of global cleansing. Then, in the aftermath, between 2012 and 2020, O'Dea sees a time of great collective healing. In other words, the global breakdown will be followed by a time of global breakthrough.

## 12.21.12—Just Another Day

The first five views of 2012 all involve some kind of massive cataclysm and/or grand rebirth of the planet and human enlightenment. The sixth view, the one I hold, is that 2012 will bring neither global catastrophe nor global enlightenment. The year 2012, like any year, may bring its share of unexpected disasters and challenges, but there is no credible evidence to suggest that the end of the world as we know it or some quantum leap in consciousness will occur. Yes, the Mayan calendar will reach its end on 12.21.12, but no one knows for sure what that means, if anything. The vast majority of scientists, archaeologists, and anthropologists reject the 2012 doomsday theory.

David Friedel, an archaeologist at Washington University in St. Louis, says, "The year 2012 is nothing more than the resetting of a clock, an odometer reaching zero before it starts again." Karl Kruszelnicki says, "...when a calendar comes to the end of a cycle, it just rolls over into the next cycle. In our Western society, every year 31 December is followed, not by the End of the World, but by 1 January. So 13.0.0.0.0 in the Mayan calendar will be followed by 0.0.0.0.1—or good-ol' 22 December 2012, with only a few shopping days left to Christmas."[43]

End date 2012 simply doesn't hold up to serious scrutiny. Anne Pyburn, an anthropologist at Indiana University who studies the Maya, says bluntly, "I don't pay any attention to this stuff because it's bunk."[44]

The year 2012 will undoubtedly hold its share of surprises, but don't get caught up in the end-of-the-world hysteria or panic. Even the committed 2012 followers can't agree on what's going to happen. Their theories range from the end of the world to some new plane of awareness. There's a pretty big difference between all-out apocalypse and a new level of spiritual awareness. Any alleged event with such divergent, wide-ranging scenarios should immediately be viewed with a healthy dose of skepticism and caution.

The Bible specifically warns against being taken captive by this kind of New Age mysticism: "See to it that no one takes you captive through philosophy and empty deception, according to the tradition of men, according to the elementary principles of the world, rather than according to Christ" (Colossians 2:8). It's interesting to me that when Jesus gave His final great discourse to His disciples He listed many of the key signs of the end times, and the very first thing He said was, "See to it that no one misleads you" (Matthew 24:4). The chief sign of the times is surging deception. I believe that the New Age 2012 eschatology is a part of this deception.

## PLUS ULTRA

At one time, Spain controlled both sides of the narrowest point of the Strait of Gibraltar. According to ancient tradition, at that narrowing of the two land masses (Africa and Europe), there were two huge pillars erected here by Hercules—hence they were called the Pillars of Hercules. Prior to Columbus' voyage in 1492, these pillars were said to mark the end of the world, described by a three-word Latin saying: *NE PLUS ULTRA,* which, translated, means, "No more beyond." The notion of "No More Beyond" was the standard belief of that time. No one would dare question the prevailing conviction that the western horizon contained nothing new. After Columbus' discovery of a new world beyond Spain, recognition of the revised outlook was pressed into Spanish colonial coins. Coins featuring the Pillars of Hercules were struck with a simple Latin slogan, *PLUS ULTRA,* which meant "More Beyond."[45]

Many today are predicting that December 21, 2012 is *NE PLUS ULTRA,* but I believe it's *PLUS ULTRA.* There is more beyond. It's not the end. But what does the future hold?

Can we know what's coming?

4

# THE LOST BOOK
# OF NOSTRADAMUS

Peering into the Crystal Ball

"After there is great trouble among mankind, a greater one is prepared.
The great mover of the universe will renew time, rain, blood, thirst,
famine, steel weapons and disease. In the heavens, a fire seen."

NOSTRADAMUS

Nostradamus.
Just the mention of his name conjures images of gloom and doom. He is unquestionably the king of secular doomsday seers. Michel de Nostredame, better known as Nostradamus, was born in St. Remy, Provence, France in 1503 and died in 1566. He came from a long line of Jewish doctors and scholars. The family converted to Christianity in 1502. Nostradamus was an apothecary (a medieval pharmacist) as well as a popular astronomer and seer. His best-known book is *Les Propheties* (*The Prophecies*). "Nostradamus began to write his prophetic verses in the city of Salon, in 1554. They are divided into ten sections called Centuries (which refers to the number of verses in each section, not to

a unit of 100 years). The Centuries were published in 1555 and 1558, and have been in print continuously ever since."[1]

The famous predictions Nostradamus recorded are written in a coded format named *quatrains,* which are mysterious verses or poems with four lines.

During Nostradamus' lifetime the Black Death, or bubonic plague, wiped out over a quarter of Europe. Writing against this backdrop undoubtedly accounts for much of the gloomy tone and apocalyptic terror that fills Nostradamus' quatrains.

To come up with his predictions, he used a technique called "scrying" (to reveal). "The technique, which is an occult practice, requires concentration on a shiny object, crystal ball, bowl of water, mirror, etc. until normal vision recedes and other visions are seen. Nostradamus used bowls of water. He surrounded his writing table with candles and waiting with quill and ink while he gazed into the bowl...Nostradamus had visions, which he translated into words."[2]

There's a familiar story that Nostradamus even predicted his own death. According to the legend, on July 1, 1566, when his assistant wished him goodnight, Nostradamus responded, "You will not find me alive at sunrise." He was found dead on July 2, 1566. While this story adds to the Nostradamus mystery, there's no way to validate whether it is true.

Since his death, Nostradamus has been acclaimed by many as a seer without peer. His writings, while interesting, are very difficult to follow. The visions he received evidently did not occur in chronological order, so they are random and very difficult to place in any context. His work is definitely not an uplifting read. Most of Nostradamus' quatrains deal with devastation and disasters, such as plagues, earthquakes, wars, floods, invasions, murders, droughts, famines, and battles. Many believe that he predicted Hitler's name (although he was off by one letter) and a description of the Nazi swastika; the discoveries of penicillin, nuclear energy, and the AIDS virus; the demise of communism; the assassination of President John F. Kennedy; and...the end of the world in 2012![3] Is Nostradamus reliable? Should we look to his prophecies for important clues about doomsday?

## Prophet of the New World Age?

Here are a few examples of Nostradamus' quatrains and what they allegedly predicted. You be the judge.[4]

Quatrain 1-29 is often viewed as a prediction of land-sea vehicles in World War II:

> When the fish that travels over both land and sea
> Is cast up on to the shore by a great wave,
> Its shape foreign, smooth and frightful.
> From the sea the enemies soon reach the walls.

### The Atom Bomb

Quatrain 2-6 is said to describe the two atom bombs dropped on Hiroshima and Nagasaki:

> Near the gates and within two cities
> There will be two scourges the like of which was
>     never seen,
> Famine within plague, people put out by steel,
> Crying to the great immortal God for relief.

The only similarity to Hiroshima and Nagasaki is "two cities" and "two scourges the like of which was never seen." However, there is no evidence of famine or plague associated with the dropping of the atom bombs. The mention of two cities and a terrible scourge is hardly enough to classify the quatrain as a legitimate prophecy.

### The Rise of Hitler

Many believe that Nostradamus anticipated the rise of three great Antichrists and that Adolf Hitler was one of them. Quatrain 3-35 is often connected with Hitler:

> From the very depths of the West of Europe,
> A young child will be born of poor people,
> He who by his tongue will seduce a great troop:
> His fame will increase towards the realm of the East.

Quatrain 2-24 is one of the most chilling prophecies. Followers of Nostradamus point to this quatrain as one of their proof texts for his accuracy. They maintain that "Hister" is a coded reference to Hitler.

> Beasts ferocious from hunger will swim across rivers:
> The greater part of the region will be against
>    the Hister,
> The great one will cause it to be dragged in an
>    iron cage,
> When the German child will observe nothing.

But what about this Hitler prophecy? Simply put, like the rest of Nostradamus' prophecies, it is vague, and does not specifically refer to Hitler at all. His name, assuming that's what was intended, isn't even spelled correctly. The original document refers to "Hister sera," not Hitler. In Quatrain 2-24, Nostradamus talks about conflict, division, strife, and war. He also mentions the area in and around Germany, which, of course, has been the site of countless battles and conflicts throughout history. Another key problem is that "Hister sera" almost certainly does not refer to a person at all, but to a place. As Tom Harris notes, "In Nostradamus' time, for example, 'Hister' referred to a geographical region near the Danube river. Most likely, skeptics argue, Nostradamus was referring to this area, not to a person. (Hitler was in fact born near the Danube River, so many believers actually embrace this interpretation)."[5] Those who want to see Hitler in this "prophecy" are not dissuaded by the facts.

By way of stark contrast, consider the reliability of the prophecies in the Bible. The Hebrew prophet Isaiah wrote during the golden age of the Hebrew prophets. Writing in about 700 B.C., he mentioned the Medo-Persian king Cyrus by name about 100 years before he was born and almost 150 years before he rose to power. "It is I who says of Cyrus, 'He is My shepherd! And he will perform all My desire.' And he declares of Jerusalem, 'She will be built,' and of the temple, 'Your foundation will be laid.' Thus says the LORD to Cyrus His anointed, whom I have taken by the right hand, to subdue nations before him" (Isaiah 44:28– 45:1).[6] Cyrus is clearly referred to in Isaiah 41:2,25, but here he is specifically named. Isaiah 45:2-6 goes on to predict the conquests of Cyrus. That is just one example of the vast difference between the specific prophecies of the Bible and the vague pronouncements of Nostradamus. We'll look at the reliability of biblical prophecies in more detail in chapter 8.

### Aftermath of World War II

Attempts have been made to equate Quatrain 1-63 with the aftermath of World War II:

> Pestilences extinguished, the world becomes smaller,
> for a long time the lands will be inhabited peacefully.
> People will travel safely through the sky (over) land

and seas:
then wars will start up again.

While some of the references in this quatrain could fit the post-World War II era, the peace didn't last "a long time" and pestilences (diseases) were not extinguished.

## Saddam Hussein

Quatrain 2-62 is viewed as a prophecy about the Antichrist that some believe was fulfilled in Saddam Hussein:

Mabus then will soon die, there will come
Of people and beasts a horrible rout:
Then suddenly one will see vengeance,
Hundred, hand, thirst, hunger when the comet will run.

Because Nostradamus saw his prophecies reflected in a bowl of water, it's maintained that *Mabus* spells *Saddam* backwards. Never mind that it actually spells *Subam*. And never mind that Saddam was not the final Antichrist. He was hanged in total disgrace in Iraq by his enemies. If this prophecy refers to some future Antichrist, it's far too vague to make any certain identification of who it points to.

## July 1999

One of the most captivating prophecies from Nostradamus for our generation is Century 10, quatrain 72, which specifically mentions the year 1999. This is one of only a few of Nostradamus' quatrains that names an actual date, and it gives the year (1999) and the month (July). It's interesting that one of the rare mentions of a specific date refers to a year near the end of the twentieth century. Here's what the quatrain says:

The year 1999, seventh month,
From the sky will come a great King of Terror:
To bring back to life the great King of the Mongols,
Before and after Mars to reign by good luck.

There are all kinds of suggestions as to the fulfillment of this prophecy. Some say it has to do with a solar eclipse that was visible throughout much of Europe on August 11, 1999. But August is not the seventh month. Close does not count in prophecy. This is one alleged prophecy of Nostradamus that we can prove was not fulfilled because we were alive when something earth-shattering—maybe even the end of the world—was supposed to occur, but did not.

## September 11, 2001

One of Nostradamus' most famous quatrains in recent time is 1-87. Many allege that he prophesied the destruction of the twin towers of the World Trade Center on September 11, 2001. According to many, this is what quatrain 1-87 says:

Earthshaking fire from the center of the earth
Will cause the towers of the New City to shake:
Two great rocks will war for a long time,
And then Arethsua shall color a new river red.

Another quatrain that is linked to 9/11 is Quatrain 6-97:

The sky will burn at forty-five degrees latitude
Fire approaches the great new city
Immediately a huge, scattered flame leaps up
When they want to have verification from the Normans
[French].

But Quatrain 1-87 actually says:

Earthshaking fire from the center of the earth
will cause tremors around the New City.
Two great rocks will war for a long time,
then Arethusa will redden a new river.

It takes a very fertile imagination to see any relation between these lines and 9/11. The only possible connections are "fire" and "New City." This highlights a couple of very serious problems with the prophecies of Nostradamus. First, there are many alleged translations of his work all over the Internet that differ greatly from on another and, in some cases, appear to even be "doctored" to better fit the proposed fulfillment of the prophecy. Second, as you can surely see, his prophecies are very vague and general, allowing people to read almost whatever meaning they want into the text. Thus, they are useless for verifying specific fulfillments. These quatrains are so vague they could be used to "fulfill" hundreds of events since the time they were written. And even if Nostradamus did make a successful prediction or two, it's not because he knew the future but due to the simple fact that anyone who "predicts" enough future events is bound to get one right eventually. Like the old saying states, "Even a clock that doesn't work is right twice a day."

The most compelling argument against Nostradamus' powers is that his apparent "hits" are the result of random chance and creative interpretation. There are about a thousand quatrains, most containing more than one prediction and all but a few described in vague, obscure terms. Over the course of hundreds of years, it's certainly possible that some events would line up with some predictions, simply by coincidence. In fact, Nostradamus may have phrased his prophecies with exactly this in mind. Most quatrains refer to deaths, wars, or natural disasters—events that are sure to occur again and again throughout history...This imprecise language does lend itself well to subjective interpretation—when the exact meaning is unclear, it's easy to plug in one's own experiences to reach some sort of understanding.

This is a lot like modern horoscopes. Horoscopes typically detail things a wide range of people experience regularly, such as "conflicts at work," "happiness in relationships" or "exciting new changes." Chances are, these predictions will line up with your life, at least some of the time.[7]

Some argue that the reason Nostradamus' quatrains are so vague is that he saw things in the future that he was unable to describe using language from his own day. While this could account for a few of the generalities, there is little, and often nothing, in any of these prophecies that even remotely refers to the alleged fulfillments in modern times. Nostradamus' name can be added to the long list of false prophets in history.

## Nostradamus and 2012

Many recent reports allege that there is a lost book of Nostradamus that has recently come to light. According to one Nostradamus Web site,

In 1994, Italian journalist Enza Massa was at the Italian National Library in Rome when she stumbled upon an unusual find. It was a manuscript dating to 1629, titled: Nostradamus Vatinicia Code. Michel de Notredame, the author's name, was on the inside in indelible ink. This manuscript, never published by Nostradamus, was handed down to the prophet's son and later donated by him to

Pope Urban VIII. It did not surface again until now, almost four hundred years later.

The cryptic paintings vary from the strange to the bizarre, with images of popes, decapitations and strange creatures. Known as the "Vaticinia Nostradami," this book has often been considered to be Nostradamus' final prophecies regarding the end of the world as we know it.[8]

I saw a program in 2008 on the History Channel titled "The Lost Book of Nostradamus and 2012." The gist of the program is that the last book of Nostradamus has recently been discovered and analyzed. According to the documentary, this lost book contains seven stark images, tables, or enigmatic drawings that, according to experts, tell a story that points to a coming apocalypse in 2012. They are viewed as a detailed account of a crisis in 2012. A wheel that appears at the top of the images, known as the "wheel of time," could be dubbed the original "wheel of fortune." To view excellent color photographs of the drawings, go to "The Lost Book of Nostradamus" at www.mendhak.com/40 -the-lost-book-of-nostradamus.aspx.

As these drawings were shown on the History Channel, my first impression was that, like Nostradamus' writings, they are subject to all kinds of interpretations. One can almost read whatever he wants into them. Look at them for yourself and see if they point clearly to 2012 as the date of the end of the world. Frankly, I can't figure out any consistent, coherent message from them. The problem for those who try to build their 2012 case on these etchings is that each presupposition and conclusion is built on a previous one. If just a single one of the long series of imaginative interpretations is incorrect, the entire scheme falls like a house of cards.

## False Prophets Beware!

It's critical for us to remember that the Bible strictly forbids the kind of divination and fortune-telling that Nostradamus practiced. What he engaged in was not a harmless, innocuous, or even entertaining practice—it was divination, which is explicitly condemned in the Bible. Consider these words from Scripture:

> There shall not be found among you anyone who makes his son or his daughter pass through the fire, one who uses divination, one who practices witchcraft, or one who interprets omens, or a sorcerer, or one who casts a spell, or a medium, or a spiritist, or one who calls up the dead. For whoever does these things is detestable to the Lord; and because of these detestable things the Lord your God will drive them out before you (Deuteronomy 18:10-12).

> When a prophet speaks in the name of the Lord, if the thing does not come about or come true, that is the thing which the Lord has not spoken. The prophet has spoken presumptuously; you shall not be afraid of him (Deuteronomy 18:22; see also Isaiah 47:13-14; Jeremiah 27:9; Revelation 21:8).

Those who traffic in divination, spiritism, sorcery, and other occult practices are explicitly warned by God, and we are commanded not to listen to their presumptuous prophecies.

## The All-time Bestseller

As you can see, I don't put any stock in Nostradamus' prophecies or any purported prophecy he made about 2012; in fact, I believe they are false prophecies derived from the unbiblical practices of divination and sorcery.

If we want to find clear, reliable prophecies about 2012, we will have to look elsewhere. But where? How about the bestselling book of all time, the Bible? Does it have anything to say about the end of the world in 2012?

Many believe that it does!

# BIBLE CODES, THE BOOK OF REVELATION, AND ARMAGEDDON

## Is 2012 in the Bible?

"For three thousand years a code in the Bible has remained hidden. Now it has been unlocked by computer—and it may reveal our future...the code may warn of unprecedented danger yet to come—perhaps the real Apocalypse."

MICHAEL DROSNIN (*THE BIBLE CODE*)

"Is the Bible Code the 'map' that describes the cycles, as well as the seed events that set in motion all the human dramas playing out across our world today?"

GREGG BRADEN (*FRACTAL TIME*)

The word *eschatology* means "study of the last" or "last things." Every major religion has some kind of eschatology or teaching about how everything is going to finally end up. For many Muslims, it's the coming of their Mahdi or Messiah, who will convert the world to Islam and rule in peace and prosperity. Buddhists reject the idea of a definitive end of all things; rather, they envision endless cycles of life and death that can ultimately lead to Nirvana, a state of complete awakening. Like Buddhists, Hindus also view time in cycles and believe that we are living in the "age of darkness," the last of four periods that constitute the current age. Most Hindus believe that the world will ultimately be destroyed in an apocalypse and then recreated.

Many today are familiar with the view of Christian eschatology presented in the best-selling *Left Behind* fiction series. Many are familiar with words and phrases such as *rapture, Tribulation, Antichrist, the second coming of Christ, millennium, the final judgment,* and *hell* and *heaven.* All orthodox Christians believe in a literal second coming of Jesus to earth, the bodily resurrection of all people, and a final judgment.

The 2012 phenomenon is the New Age eschatology. It's their answer to how the world will end, or at least how the world as we know it will end and usher in a new stage of collective consciousness. Most religions and cultures past and present have some kind of doomsday or end-time scenario. The New Age movement has adopted the Mayan calendar as the centerpiece for its view of how this world will end and the next one, if there is one, will begin. The startlingly unique feature of the Mayan doomsday prophecy, and the New Age eschatology, is that it names the specific date for the end: December 21, 2012.

The ancient Mayans point to December 21, 2012 as the end, or possibly a new beginning. But they are far from alone in predicting an end of the world as we know it. Other ancient texts point to an end of the world and the coming of a great deliverer. For example, Shiite Muslims are waiting for the arrival of the Twelfth Imam, or Mahdi, who will usher in a time of worldwide prosperity and peace. Christians look for the second coming of Jesus Christ.

In the Bible, there are many New Testament passages that refer to the end times. Even Jesus prophesied great turmoil and upheaval for the world in the final years of this age. For example:

> You will be hearing of wars and rumors of wars. See that you are not frightened, for those things must take place, but that is not yet the end. For nation will rise against nation, and kingdom against kingdom, and in various places there will be famines and earthquakes. But all these things are merely the beginning of birth pangs (Matthew 24:6-8).

> He continued by saying to them, "Nation will rise against nation and kingdom against kingdom, and there will be great earthquakes, and in various places plagues and famines; and there will be terrors and great signs from heaven" (Luke 21:10-11).

Given the abundance of passages about the last days, does the Bible have anything specific to say about 2012? Some claim it does. Gregg Braden, a noted 2012ologist, says, "The Bible Code offers yet another example of an ancient message that identifies 2012 as the gateway of opportunity."[1] Lawrence Joseph, in his book *Apocalypse 2012,* confidently states, "The Bible tells us that God will annihilate the earth in 2012."[2] Let's examine the evidence for such bold assertions.

## What Are Bible Codes?

According to Michael Drosnin, the Bible code was discovered by Dr. Eliyahu Rips, a leading mathematician and expert in group theory.[3] The basic tenet underlying the whole Bible code phenomenon is that there are hidden, cryptic codes in the Hebrew text of the Old Testament—"a Bible beneath the Bible"—that can be discovered by using computers to search for the letters of specific words that occur at a specific interval or spacing. The process is referred to as "equidistant letter sequencing" (ELS), or the "skip" process. As Old Testament scholar Richard Taylor notes,

> The basic concept behind the Bible code theory is relatively simple. If one takes the Hebrew text of the Torah... and deletes all spaces and punctuation between words and verses, this creates a continuous strand of text consisting of 304,805 letters. One can then search that text for encoded messages found by skipping a certain equal number of letters in the Biblical text in order to isolate the letters of a particular word being sought.[4]

In other words, the sequencer finds a Hebrew letter, skips ten letters, finds the next Hebrew letter, then skips ten more letters, and continues this process until the "hidden" word is revealed. The skip can be of any length as long as the skips are equal, and the word can be spelled forward, backward, vertically, horizontally, or diagonally.

## Code Read

Proponents of the 2012 doomsday view rely on *The Bible Code* by Michael Drosnin to support their thesis. In this bestseller, Drosnin claims to have decoded all kinds of events that have already occurred and some that still lie in the future. In the foreword to the book, Drosnin claims,

> For three thousand years a code in the Bible has remained hidden. Now it has been unlocked by computer—and it may reveal our future. Events that happened thousands of years after the Bible was written—World War II, the Moon landing, Watergate, both Kennedy assassinations, the election of Bill Clinton, the Oklahoma City bombing—all

were foretold in the code...And the code may warn of unprecedented danger yet to come—perhaps the real apocalypse.[5]

Drosnin points specifically to 2012 as an ominous, even terminal year. According to Drosnin, the words *earth annihilated* correspond to the year 2012 (the year 5772 in the Hebrew calendar). Drosnin makes these startling forecasts: "The Bible code warns that a collision with the earth may be a real danger...Other probabilities are encoded. Both '5570' and '5772'—the years 2010 and 2012—also appear with 'comet.' 'Days of horror' runs across 2010. 'Darkness' and 'gloom' cross 'comet' right below. 'Earth annihilated' states the hidden text right above the year 2012."[6]

Is there any substance to Drosnin's predictions? Should we look to hidden Bible codes for information about the end of days? Gregg Braden has bought into the Bible code phenomenon. "Vertically, horizontally, and diagonally, the names of countries, events, dates, times, and people intersect with one another in a way that sets the Bible apart from any other text, giving us a snapshot into the events of our past and window into our future."[7] Is he right?

## Breaking the Bible Code

Back in the early 1990s a Jewish man from Hollywood called me on the phone to ask me if I knew anything about codes that were hidden in the Old Testament. When I confessed my ignorance on this subject, he offered to send me a video about it. The video featured a teaching session conducted by a Jewish rabbi on various codes that he claimed were hidden in the text of the Old Testament. The rabbi's presentation was long, tedious, and boring.

So I threw away the video and forgot all about Bible codes. Little did I know that a few years later the matter of Bible codes would become a big issue.

In the late 1990s there was an explosion of popular books dealing with hidden codes in the Bible. These books were written by Jewish rabbis, Messianic Jews, and Bible prophecy teachers. The best known of these books is Michael Drosnin's *The Bible Code*, which was a runaway bestseller when it was released in 1997. The book was such a success that a sequel, *Bible Code II: The Countdown,* was released a few years later. A movie titled *The Omega Code* used the unraveling of hidden Bible codes as the key to its end-time plot.

Bible code enthusiasts claim to have found references to Hitler, the Holocaust, the assassinations of John F. Kennedy and Israeli Prime Minister Yitzhak Rabin, Princess Diana, the Gulf War, man's landing on the moon, and many references to *Yeshua* (Jesus) in Messianic passages.

While this sounds intriguing, the whole notion of Bible codes should be approached with great caution for seven main reasons. First, some of the skip distances can be up to 1000 letters. The use of such large skips to find letters that comprise an alleged code makes this whole process suspect.

Second, in the Torah alone (the first five books of the Old Testament), using the ELS process, scholars have found 2328 references to Mohammed, 104 references to Krishna, and the name Koresh (as in David Koresh) encoded 2729 times.[8]

Third, the uniqueness of these codes to Scripture is yet to be proven. One of the key arguments of Bible code enthusiasts is that the existence of these supposedly hidden codes validates the uniqueness and inspiration of Scripture. However, many excellent Bible scholars strongly contend that these codes are much ado about nothing. The principles used for finding codes in the Bible have also been used on other books, and references to world figures and events have been found in these secular writings as well. One can use the same techniques on other books and get the same kinds of "hits" Drosnin documents in *The Bible Code*. Drosnin issued this challenge: "When my critics find a message about the assassination of a prime minister encrypted in *Moby Dick,* I will believe them."[9] Accepting that challenge, and using the same ELS techniques, Professor Brendan McKay, a mathematician at the Australian National University, searched Herman Melville's *Moby Dick* for encrypted messages. He discovered 13 predicted assassinations of public figures, including Indira Gandhi, Martin Luther King, Sirhan Sirhan, John F. Kennedy, Abraham Lincoln, and Yitzhak Rabin. Bar-Natan and McKay have demonstrated that names such as *Hitler* and *Nazi* can easily be discovered in English translations of *War and Peace* as well as the King James Version of Genesis, the first book of the Bible.

A mathematician named David Thomas conducted an ELS search on the book of Genesis and found the words *code* and *bogus* close together 60 times. Does this prove the Bible code is bogus? Thomas performed an ELS analysis on Drosnin's second book, *Bible Code II: The Countdown,* and discovered the message "The Bible Code is a silly, dumb, fake, false, evil, nasty, dismal fraud and snake-oil hoax."[10]

Fourth, there is absolutely no biblical support for the practice of finding codes hidden in the Bible. Neither Jesus nor the apostles ever did such, even though they quoted or alluded to the Old Testament hundreds of times. Of course, they didn't have computers, but that raises another issue: You have to have a computer to find these hidden messages, and until just a few decades ago computers were unavailable. Why would God hide all this information in codes that no one could access until very recently?

Fifth, even if these hidden codes were for real, they will not provide any information about the last days. The whole Bible code explosion is an exercise in "Monday morning quarterbacking." All the "messages" found so far deal only with what we already know in hindsight. We already know about Hitler and John F. Kennedy, and if a person is a Christian, he already knows that Jesus is the Messiah. The only way these codes can possibly be validated is after the fact, and if something is "proven" only after it has already happened, then it is no longer a future event. For this reason, "most of those who consider themselves serious code researchers (including Doron Witztum, Eliyahu Rips, Yoav Rosenberg, and Harold Gans) have now publicly distanced themselves from Drosnin and other 'amateurs' who are using Bible Codes to allegedly predict the future."[11]

Sixth, the Bible is filled with straightforward prophecies. We would be much better off turning to these passages and studying their clear meaning rather than attempting to find things out through hidden codes. J. Paul Tanner provides a helpful warning:

> People do not need some "biblical crossword puzzle." Instead they need to read and meditate on the revealed truths of God's holy Word. They need to be engaged in Bible study to learn the marvelous truths God has revealed, rather than being diverted by the speculative counting of letters (for which there is no divine sanction or apostolic precedent).[12]

Dr. Richard Taylor agrees.

> In approaching Bible study this way, Scripture becomes

an amorphous collection of letters with an almost infinite number of combinations based on ELSs that run sometimes forward, sometimes backward, sometimes vertically, and sometimes diagonally. Bible study is thus reduced to discovering what one sets out to find rather than listening patiently to what the divine author has to say in and through the text. Is there a code to be found in the Bible? Is it through mathematical computations or mystical combinations of letters separated sometimes by vast distances that God has chosen to reveal himself and his plan for the universe? I think not. The combinations of letters and so-called messages discovered by Bible code researchers appear to be contrived and/or coincidental. I do not believe that there is a code to be found in the Bible.[13]

Seventh, while 2012 enthusiasts point to the reliability of Bible codes to predict the future, they cannot pass the test. For 2012 experts, Bible codes are a "3,000-year-old map of time."[14] Gregg Braden confidently contends that "there is about a 1-in-200,000 chance that the information revealed in the Bible Code is a coincidence."[15] He says that the Bible code accurately predicted "events ranging from World War II, the Shoemaker-Levy comet impact with Jupiter, the Scud missiles discovered during the Gulf War in Iraq, and the Kennedy assassination."[16] Braden points to the assassination of Israeli Prime Minister Yitzhak Rabin in November 1995 as another proof of the accuracy of Bible codes. "The prime minister's name, Rabin, had been spelled out, along with the date of the assassination, the name of the city it would occur within, and even the assassin's name: Amir."[17]

Based on these conclusions, Braden and many others maintain that the ancient matrix in the Bible codes is a reliable guide for peering into the future and that it points to 2012 as the end.

In spite of such claims, the most damaging evidence against using Bible codes to predict the future is that they have already been proven to be false. At least two predictions made ahead of time in 1997 were erroneous. Drosnin predicted a nuclear war, world war, or Armageddon in 2000 or 2006, and a comet strike on the earth in 2006.[18]

In *Bible Code II: The Countdown,* Drosnin claimed that some kind of final countdown began on September 11, 2001. He maintained that the phrases "Atomic Holocaust," "World War," and "End of Days" all appear in the same year—2006. He said the odds against this happening by chance are 100,000 to 1.[19] After predicting 2006 as doomsday, Drosnin gave himself an "out" by saying, "The Bible Code is not a prediction that we will all die in 2006. It is warning that all *might* die in 2006, if we do not change our future" or "find a way to survive."[20] The year 2006 is now history. The end did not come, as Drosnin prognosticated. But what great change did mankind supposedly make to avert the disaster? Drosnin has never told us. Despite his attempted disclaimer, this is another sensational Bible code "prediction" that failed to materialize.

None of what Drosnin predicted for 2006 happened. According to the Bible, anyone who attempts to predict the future and is not 100 percent accurate is a false prophet (Deuteronomy 18:20-22). The Bible has a proven track record of predicting the future perfectly for more than two millennia. Drosnin's "hitting streak" didn't last a decade. So, how can the Bible code be part of God's revelation to man if it doesn't meet His perfect standard for predicting the future?

As you can see, I'm not a fan of using Bible codes in an attempt to predict the future. Bible codes are totally unreliable for predicting the future, including any events related to 2012 or the end of the world. If you search long enough and make the skips between letters far enough apart, you can find just about anything you want to find.

## 2012 and the Tribulation

Some 2012ologists, in their quest for biblical support for doomsday 2012, point to words from the biblical prophets. For example, Isaiah 24 is quoted as referring to the solar pole flip in 2012:

> Behold, the LORD lays the earth waste, devastates it, distorts its surface, and scatters its inhabitants...The earth will be completely laid waste and completely despoiled... The earth is broken asunder, the earth is split through, the earth is shaken violently. The earth reels to and fro like a drunkard, and it totters like a shack, for its transgression is heavy upon it, and it will fall, never to rise again (Isaiah 24:1,3,19-20).

The prophet Joel is also cited by some:

> For the day of the LORD is coming; surely it is near, a day of darkness and gloom, a day of clouds and thick darkness...I will display wonders in the sky and on the earth, blood, fire and columns of smoke. The sun will be turned into darkness and the moon into blood before the great and awesome day of the LORD (Joel 2:1-2,30-31).

2012 enthusiasts maintain that the Old Testament prophecies of the end-time Great Tribulation are consistent with what will happen during the polar shift they expect in 2012. They also point to graphic passages in the book of Revelation:

> I looked when He broke the sixth seal, and there was a great earthquake; and the sun became black as sackcloth made of hair, and the whole moon became like

blood; and the stars of the sky fell to the earth, as a fig tree casts its unripe figs when shaken by a great wind. The sky was split apart like a scroll when it is rolled up, and every mountain and island were moved out of their places. Then the kings of the earth and the great men and the commanders and the rich and the strong and every slave and free man hid themselves in the caves and among the rocks of the mountains; and they said to the mountains and to the rocks, "Fall on us and hide us from the presence of Him who sits on the throne, and from the wrath of the Lamb" (Revelation 6:12-16).

To many 2012 researchers, this upheaval sounds a lot like pole reversal. The trumpet judgments in Revelation 8 are also cited as proof of a major cataclysm consistent with pole reversal, solar flares, and Nibiru hitting the earth:

The angel took the censer and filled it with the fire of the altar, and threw it to the earth; and there followed peals of thunder and sounds and flashes of lightning and an earthquake. And the seven angels who had the seven trumpets prepared themselves to sound them. The first sounded, and there came hail and fire, mixed with blood, and they were thrown to the earth; and a third of the earth was burned up, and a third of the trees were burned up, and all the green grass was burned up. The second angel sounded, and something like a great mountain burning with fire was thrown into the sea; and a third of the sea became blood, and a third of the creatures which were in the sea and had life, died; and a third of the ships were destroyed. And the third angel sounded, and a great star fell from heaven, burning like a torch, and it fell on a third of the rivers and on the springs of waters. The name of the star is called Wormwood; and a third of the waters became wormwood, and many men died

from the waters, because they were made bitter. The
fourth angel sounded, and a third of the sun and a third
of the moon and a third of the stars were struck, so that
a third of them would be darkened and the day would
not shine for a third of it, and the night in the same way
(Revelation 8:5-12).

To 2012ologists, this looks like a serious case of pole reversal.
Could they be right? It is true that the Old Testament prophets
and the book of Revelation look ahead to a time of great global
conflagration when the people on earth will be punished for their
sin. Both the 2012 theory and the Bible predict catastrophic chaos
in the future. But the fact their predictions are somewhat similar
doesn't mean they are referring to the same events. In the Bible,
the events of the coming Tribulation are never related to any specific date or natural phenomenon such as polar shift.

What's more, the end-time disasters described in the book of
Revelation and by the biblical prophets will be caused by God,
not man. Much of the suffering, destruction, and trouble we
see in the world today is the result of the wrath of sinful man
and Satan. But during the Tribulation, God Himself will pour
out His wrath on a sinful, rebellious world. All 19 of the Tribulation judgments listed in Revelation are from the hand of the
Almighty.[21] While God may use natural phenomenon to bring
these judgments about, there's no mistaking that He's the One
behind them all. Even the people on earth during the Tribulation will know this (Revelation 6:16; 16:11).

Also, the judgments detailed in the book of Revelation won't
bring about the end of the world. While it is true that at least
one-half of the earth's inhabitants will die during the Tribulation, about one-half will survive.

## Consistent Interpretation

Many 2012ologists look to Bible codes and select passages in the Old Testament and the book of Revelation in an effort to support their hypothesis. Yet they fail to read the rest of the Bible, especially the book of Revelation, and take its message to heart. Their pick-and-choose method of interpretation and application is not consistent with sound scholarship. Most 2012 researchers appear to reject the clear teachings of the Bible and opt for a kind of New Age mysticism, yet at the same time they resort to allegedly hidden Bible codes to support their view of 2012. The Bible is consulted and considered reliable when they believe it supports their 2012 theory, but when it contradicts and challenges their beliefs it is rejected and in some cases even ridiculed.

While none of us are perfectly consistent in this life, one should at least make a good-faith attempt to be consistent in the use of the Bible or any other text. If people are going to use the Bible as an authoritative source to prove that doomsday 2012 is coming, they should also eagerly submit their minds and lives to the God who can predict the future.

The book of Revelation ends with Jesus Christ being proclaimed as King of kings and Lord of lords and with those who reject Him being cast into the lake of fire. That should serve as a sobering wake-up call to all who think about the future and their final destiny.

Lawrence Joseph, in his book *Apocalypse 2012*, says, "The Bible Code provides the most profound scientific evidence yet that the Bible was divinely inspired. The work of the Israeli mathematicians Rips, Witzum, and Rosenberg has withstood all scientific challenges thus far. The good news is that the book upon which so much of the world's religious faith is based has received unprecedented mathematical substantiation."[22] If the Bible is divinely inspired, and I firmly agree that it is, then we should give the plain language in the book of Revelation much more weight and credence than we give to alleged hidden Bible codes.[23]

The book of Revelation (Greek, *apokalupsis*, which means "unveiling") is about the unveiling of Jesus Christ. It's not about Mayan timetables, hidden codes, or reaching some higher level of human consciousness on our own. It's about God's judgment of this sinful world, the fall of the kingdom of man, and the ultimate triumph of Jesus Christ as King of kings and Lord of lords when He returns to earth. The book is God's infallible revelation to us of the future of planet earth.

## One Final Piece to the 2012 Puzzle

Before we delve further into our investigation of what the future holds, we need to consider one more reason many people believe the world will end in 2012. This reason has to do with a machine we all depend on every day: the computer.

Could computers hold the key to doomsday 2012?

# COMPUTERS AND 2012

## The Web Bot Project

"The Web Bot project: A tool used to speed-read the Internet web in order to find patterns or waves of behaviour. This tool is believed to be able to forecast the future based on the web surfing habits of the information generation."

2012 PREDICTIONS REVIEW

"When the Mayan calendar end date is used as a key word, there is only one Web Bot prediction. It predicts a pole shift in 2012."

SYNTHIA ANDREWS AND COLIN ANDREWS

Computers have changed the world. But what we've seen up to now is merely a faint foreshadow of what's coming. Superfast computers are now online that have processing speeds that stagger the imagination. The world's fastest computer, nicknamed Roadrunner, reached a monumental milestone on May 26, 2008 at 3:30 a.m. The $133 million IBM supercomputer system at the Los Alamos National Laboratory broke the long-sought-after petaflop barrier. Like me, you're probably wondering what in the world that means. The petaflop barrier is one quadrillion calculations per second. To put it in perspective, that's 1500 calculations per second for every man, woman, and child on earth. Scientists are now shooting for the exaflop barrier. An exaflop is a million trillion calculations per second, or a quintillion. That's a thousand times faster than a petaflop. They predict that the exaflop barrier will be reached in 2019.

IBM has developed a new supercomputer they have called the Sequoia:

> With a speed of 20 petaflops—or 20,000 trillion calculations per second—the Sequoia is expected to be the most powerful supercomputer in the world, IBM said, and will be approximately 10 times faster than today's most powerful system. To put this into perspective, if each of the 6.7 billion people on Earth had a hand calculator and worked together on a massive calculation for 24 hours per day, 365 days a year, it would take 320 years to do what Sequoia will do in one hour.[1]

With this kind of technology becoming available, many believe that computers might not only help solve difficult problems, but may also possess the kind of artificial intelligence that can help forecast the future.

## The Web Bot Project

An undertaking known as the Web Bot project has been underway since the late 1990s. Its creator wishes to remain anonymous and simply calls himself "Cliff."[2] Web Bot was developed primarily to predict the fluctuations in stock prices, but has been expanded to make predictions in other arenas. How does it work?

> It relies on a system of "spiders" that "crawl" the Internet, much like a search engine, looking for particular kinds

of words…the spiders target discussion groups, trans-
lation sites, and places where regular people post a lot
of text…Whenever the spider finds a keyword, it takes a
small 2,048-byte snip of the surrounding text and sends
it to a central collection point. Over a period of time, the
"chatter points" concentrate, revealing a spike in intensity. Like the Bible Code, the technology doesn't come
out with direct messages. It gives words or phrases that
reflect people's thought processes.[3]

To put it another way, "Web bots are looking for trends with the keyword relations they find. It searches for keywords 'standing out' in a web document but also takes in consideration the content preceding and following the keyword. This data is then analyzed by a linguistic tool to determine the meaning if there's any."[4]

Sounds pretty amazing—and it is. Web Bot technology sup-posedly taps into "preconscious awareness and finds patterns before events actually occur and presumably before people are talking about them."[5] Many believe that Web Bot has predicted several events outside the stock market:

- The crash of American Airlines flight 587
- Elements of the DC sniper case
- The space shuttle Columbia disaster[6]

So, what does all this have to do with 2012? It's pretty simple. "When December 12, 2012, the Mayan end date, is employed as a key word, Web Bot spits out one, and only one, sobering pre-diction for planet earth: a cataclysmic pole shift in 2012."[7] When this is combined with the alleged prophecies of Nostradamus and Bible codes, the 2012 end date is viewed by 2012ologists as a vir-tual slam dunk for the end of the world as we know it. Could this be true? Could the computer be right?

## Not So Fast!

Before 2012 enthusiasts get too carried away with the "artificial intelligence" of modern technology and predict the rise of the machines, it's important to note the profound limitations of Web Bot. I believe there are three points that render Web Bot useless in predicting the date for the end of the world. First, while Web Bot evidently has been useful for predicting stock fluctuations and prices, we must remember that ultimately, fluctuations and prices are influenced by human behavior. This is a very different matter than predicting the end of the world (although some may equate a stock market crash with the end of the world). Human behavior cannot subconsciously make the earth's poles shift, the sun heat up, supervolcanoes erupt violently, or trigger Himalaya-engulfing tsunamis. Predicting stock prices and forecasting earth's expiration date is not an apples-to-apples comparison. Also, I would like to see how Web Bot did prior to the stock market free-fall in 2008. If Web Bot predicted that fall, it could have saved us all a lot of money.

Second, it's important to note that, according to Web Bot, the crash of American Airlines Flight 587 would result from a terrorist act, but that has never yet been proven. So Web Bot's prediction was not completely accurate. Predictions that are merely close don't count when we're talking about a possible appointment with doomsday.

Third, when you think about it, Web Bot is only as good as the information it can access on the Internet. All Web Bot does is comb the Internet for clues. I agree with the following analysis:

> I'm not seeing how a computer can figure out what's going to happen in 2012 simply by visiting Web sites published by real people. The more data Web Bots get

pointing towards 2012 just means more and more people are publishing stuff about 2012 and the end of the world. Remember, the only thing they can crawl is the Internet and what you find on the Internet was created by real persons, not God. They will surely get a strong correlation between 2012 and the end of the world; there's ton of Web sites talking about it.

So, can Web Bots predict stuff? Yes I believe it can and it's a really nice piece of technology. I'm pretty sure preventing terrorists attacks can be done using Web Bots and also predicting anything involving human interaction. Remember, it crawls the web, written by humans, so it can only predict what humans are able to predict: Just in a shorter time frame![8]

That's the profound weakness of Web Bot. It can only search what people have put into the Internet. Humans could collectively be creating a 2012 date with doomsday. One person who has evaluated Web Bot's predictive shortcomings put it very well: "Would you put your trust in a teacher or leader that was getting its education in an asylum? The asylum in this case is the entire web library. It has its moments of brilliance, but in the end it is already corrupted with less than accurate data."[9]

## Another Dead End

For these reasons, I believe that computers can be added to the growing list of unreliable predictors of end-time events. They aren't any more trustworthy than the Mayans, Nostradamus, or Bible codes. So, where do we turn?

Can anyone accurately predict history's final day?

Is there any sure word about the future? About the end of the world?

# DOES ANYBODY REALLY KNOW WHAT TIME IT IS?

## Date-setters and the End of the World

> "Our world has an expiration date. It ends at a specific time,
> with a specific event, on a day that was marked on a
> calendar more than 2,000 years ago."
>
> GREGG BRADEN

There's a story about two men talking about the end of the world. One man says to his friend, "I calculate that the end of the world will come in 217,000 years." His friend, greatly agitated, replied, "How many did you say?" The first man repeated, "217,000." The friend said with great relief, "You scared me; I thought you said 117,000."

Attempting to predict when the world will end is nothing new. This has been the subject of untold speculation. Since the beginning of time, people have tried to predict doomsday and the events associated with it. So the 2012 theorists have a lot of company. There are many others who have tried to pinpoint an exact time for earth's expiration. And the 2012ologists, like those before them, will be added to the long list in the date-setter's hall of shame when their predictions fail to materialize. Date-setters always garner attention for a while but end up embarrassed and appearing foolish when their end date comes and goes.

## The Dating Game

To illustrate the folly of date-setting, let's look at a few examples of those who have tried to predict earth's "closing time." One Web site chronicles over 200 predictions of the end of the world (and still counting).[1] Another Web site lists "30 days when the world didn't end." Here are a few of their examples with a few of my own favorites added in.[2]

**2800 B.C.:** The oldest surviving prediction of the world's imminent demise was found inscribed upon an Assyrian clay tablet which stated, "Our earth is degenerate in these latter days. There are signs that the world is speedily coming to an end. Bribery and corruption are common." Wherever more than two people over 30 are gathered together, expect to hear remarkably similar sentiments.

**Second century A.D.:** The Montanists, founded in around A.D. 155 by a man called Montanus, were perhaps the first recognizable Christian end-of-the-world cult. They believed that Christ's triumphant return was imminent and established a base in Anatolia, central Turkey, where they anxiously waited for doomsday.

**March 25, 970:** The Lotharingian computists believed they had found evidence in the Bible that a conjunction of certain feast days prefigured the end times. They were just one of a wide scattering of millennial cults that sprang up in advance of the first millennium A.D. The millennial panic endured for at least

30 years after the fateful date had come and gone, with some adjustment made so that the year 1000 was counted from the time of the crucifixion rather than the nativity.

**1284:** Pope Innocent III predicted Christ's second coming would occur in this year. He based his prediction on the date of the inception of the Muslim faith, then added 666 years to that.

**Botticelli's Mystical Nativity:** To this painting, which hangs in the National Gallery in London, Botticelli added a Greek inscription that characterized the early 1500s as a pre-apocalyptic period known as the Tribulation and anticipated a second coming in or around the year 1504.

**February 1, 1524:** Panicked by predictions made by a group of London astrologers, some 20,000 people abandoned their homes and fled to high ground in anticipation of a second great flood that was predicted to start from the Thames. Proving that this was not just the error of a London-centric media, the German astrologer Johannes Stoeffler then made a similar prediction for later in the same month.

**1648:** After close study of the kabbalah, the Turkish rabbi Sabbatai Zevi predicted that the Messiah would make a miraculous return in 1648, and that his name would be Sabbatai Zevi. When 1648 came and went without any appreciable apocalypse, Sabbatai revised his estimate.

**1666:** This year was packed with apocalyptic portent. Because the date included the number commonly accepted as the biblical number of the beast and followed a protracted period of plague in England, it was little surprise that many should believe the Great Fire of London to be a herald of the last days.

**1792:** Shakers predicted the end of the world.

**1914:** Jehovah's Witnesses have set several dates for the prophetic end—1914, 1915, 1918, 1919, 1920, 1925, 1941, 1975, and 1994.

**1844:** Baptist preacher William Miller predicted Jesus would return to upstate New York on October 22, 1844. This became known in American history as the "Great Disappointment."

**1988:** Another rash of predictions nominated this year as the world's last. There was even a major book titled *88 Reasons Why Christ Will Return in 1988*, by Edgar Whisenant. The book didn't sell too well in 1989.

**1994:** Harold Camping, in his book *Are You Ready?*, predicted the Lord's return in September 1994. The book was full of numerology that added up to September 6, 1994 as the date of Christ's return. He has recently set October 21, 2011 as the date for the end of the world.

**March–May 1997:** The year of comet Hale-Bopp gave rise to several end-of-the-world theories, all based on a mistaken observation by amateur astronomer Chuck Shramek. The Heaven's Gate cult seized on these combined rumors as their signal to commit mass suicide in March of that year. This was also said to be the 6000th anniversary of the creation, as calculated by Bishop Ussher (1581–1656), leading to another wave of last-days panic.

**A.D. 2000:** Several early church fathers believed that the earth would only last 6000 years. They made a correlation between the six days of creation and 2 Peter 3:8, which says, "With the Lord one day is like a thousand years, and a thousand years like one day." Because God rested on the seventh day, these church fathers believed the final 1000 years of history would be a Sabbath rest for the earth. Many seized upon this mistaken idea and the Y2K panic and predicted the end of the age.

**September 2008:** On the basis of certain feast days and "blood moons," some predicted the rapture would occur at this time.

The list could go on and on. But you get the point: date-setters are batting zero. The basic conclusion I've come to is that if someone sets a specific date for the end of the world, Armageddon, or the coming of Jesus Christ, you can be sure the predicted event won't happen on that day. Jesus said as much in Matthew 24:42,44: "Be on the alert, for you do not know which day your Lord is coming...For this reason you also must be ready; for the Son of Man is coming at an hour when you do not think He will" (see also Matthew 25:13; Acts 1:7). If many people believe He's coming in 2012 or that it's all over on 12.21.12, you can mark it down—that's not the day.

In spite of the clear teaching of Scripture and the miserable record of those who have tried to predict the end date, people continue to set dates for the coming of Christ and the end of the world. What's amazing is that Jesus said during His earthly ministry that He did not even know the day of His coming. "Of that day and hour no one knows, not even the angels of heaven, nor the Son, but the Father alone" (Matthew 24:36). Anyone who claims to know the specific time of Christ's coming is claiming he knows something that the Father didn't even tell the Son while He was on earth. That is the height of arrogance and folly.

## What Time Is It?

That leaves us asking this question: What time is it now? At every prophecy conference I have ever attended that had a question-and-answer session, someone has asked that question or some form of it. After all, it *is* the big question, isn't it? Where are we on God's prophetic timetable? What time is it now? There are three points that help us to arrive at a general answer for this question of the ages.

## 1. We Are Living in the Last Days

The end has already begun. The apostle Peter said all the way back in the A.D. 60s that "the end of all things is near" (1 Peter 4:7). All the way back in New Testament times, the apostles "sensed that they had moved dramatically closer to the consummation of God's plan for this world."[3] The Old Testament age had ended; they were now living in a new era. For the apostles, the end of the age was already a present reality.

The first coming of Jesus Christ inaugurated the "last days" (Acts 2:14-20; Hebrews 1:2) or the "last hour" (1 John 2:18), and His second coming will culminate the end of the age. Therefore, the entire current church age is the last days, so the end of this age could be called the last days of the last days. The reference to this age as the "last days" or "last hour" is a vivid reminder that Christ could come at any time. Every generation since the first coming of Christ has lived with the hope that it could be the terminal generation and that Christ could return at any moment. No prophetic event must be fulfilled before Christ's coming, so in this sense the end is indeed near.

## 2. God's Timetable Is Not Our Timetable

The apostle Peter reminded us that in the last days, scoffers will question the promise of Christ's return (2 Peter 3:3-4). Part of Peter's answer to these mocking skeptics is that God's view of time is very different from ours: "With the Lord one day is like a thousand years, and a thousand years like one day" (2 Peter 3:8). The reason for the apparent delay in Christ's coming is that God is waiting to give people time to turn to Him in repentance and faith. Be careful to never confuse God's delay and patience for a change in His plans. God will fulfill His promise in His time. His timetable is not our timetable.

### 3. Christ's Coming Is Closer than It's Ever Been

I'm reminded of the man who was sitting downstairs late one night reading while his wife had already retired to bed. He heard the grandfather clock begin to chime in the hallway and started counting the chimes to see what time it was. The clock chimed nine, ten, eleven, twelve, then thirteen times. Upon hearing the thirteenth bell, he got up, ran up the stairs, bolted into the bedroom to wake up his wife, and said, "Honey, wake up—it's later than it's ever been!"

That's the one sure answer I can give when people want to know what time it is. We are closer to the end than we've ever been. However, as for the specific time, no one knows for sure how close we are to the end except the Lord.

To get some idea of how close we are, we can point to various signs the Lord has given us, such as the regathering of Israel to her land, the European Union as the possible reuniting of the ancient Roman Empire, the rise of tensions in the Middle East, the unstable conditions in Russia, and the development of a one-world economy that could easily be controlled by the Antichrist. And I do believe that these signs tell us that the second coming of Christ could be very near. So the rapture must be even nearer. But how near? We really don't know. The specific day or hour of His coming is unknown. We can say, "Jesus might come today," but we must also admit that He might not come in the next decade. He might not come in my lifetime or yours.

As prophecy teacher Ed Hindson reminds us,

> God's clock, the clock of history, is ticking away. It never speeds up and never slows down. It just keeps on ticking, continually and relentlessly, moving us closer and closer to the end of the age. How close we are to the end will

only be revealed by time itself. Don't gamble with your eternal destiny. Time may very well be running out. [4]

Make sure you are ready when Jesus comes.

### Looking At the Fig Tree

One Bible passage that is often used to pinpoint or at least narrow down the time for the coming of Christ is Matthew 24:34: "I say to you, this generation will not pass away until all these things take place." Some people use this verse in an attempt to prove that once the signs of the last days begin, Christ will return within one generation, which is usually calculated to be about 40 years. However, the "generation" that would "not pass away" probably refers to the generation that will personally witness the signs described in Matthew 24:4-30—that is, the events of the Tribulation period. It is *that* generation that will not pass away before Christ returns. Thus, this verse should not be used to establish a date for the coming of Christ.

Let's look at the context of Matthew 24:34:

> Now learn the parable from the fig tree: when its branch has already become tender, and puts forth its leaves, you know that summer is near; so, you too, when you see all these things, recognize that He is near, right at the door. Truly I say to you, this generation will not pass away until all these things take place (verses 32-34).

Many believe that the fig tree here is a reference to the nation of Israel because the fig tree was used to represent Israel in the Old Testament. They say that the budding of the fig tree occurred in May 1948, when Israel became a nation. Since a generation is about 40-60 years, they expected Christ to come by 1988 or 2008. When this didn't happen, some changed the length of a generation to 80 years or changed the date of the fig tree's budding to June 1967, when the Jews took the city of Jerusalem. That extends the "generation" of Matthew 24:34 out perhaps as far as 2027, depending on how long a generation can be stretched. The constant need to change the length of a generation is further evidence of the folly of attempting to set specific dates for Christ's return.

I don't believe the fig tree in Matthew 24:32 has anything to do with the rebirth of the nation of Israel. Jesus was probably using the tree to simply make a point that anyone could understand. He was saying that just as one can tell summer is near by the blossoming of a fig tree, so those who are alive on earth during the Tribulation will be able to see that Christ's coming is near when the signs predicted in Matthew 24:4-31 begin to happen.

My grandfather was a pastor who loved Bible prophecy. When Israel became a nation in 1948, he recognized the prophetic significance of this event. My father has told me that my grandfather commented on numerous occasions that he believed Jesus would come in his lifetime. He lived his life believing the end was near and looking for the rapture. However, the Lord called my grandfather home in 1963 at the age of 63. Was my grandfather wrong? No, he wasn't wrong. He didn't miss the rapture. He is presently with the Lord, and at the rapture, he will be resurrected to join the Lord and His saints in the air.

The precious hope of the rapture added unspeakable joy to his life, and led him to live as if Jesus could come at any moment. That's what the hope of the rapture should do to all of us! We should live in anticipation of His return. Yet we must leave the timing of this event up to the Lord.

All I can say when people ask me how close we are to the end is that I earnestly believe that Jesus could come today, and that I pray that He will. That's close enough for me!

## Blind Date

The Bible never gives specific dates for any future, end-time events, let alone the end of the world. The reason for this is clear: God wants His followers to always be ready. If we knew the date of Christ's coming or the end of the world, we would be tempted to be lazy and unconcerned if it were a long way off, and frantic and hysterical if it were close at hand. By leaving the date hidden from us, God makes it necessary for us to always be ready for the consummation of the age (Matthew 24:42–25:13).

So, can we know *when* the end will come? No! We should stay far away from date-setting. It's wrong and dangerous. Date-setters are upsetters. They promote unnecessary worry, and even hysteria and panic. Jesus said no one knows when the end is coming; I'll take His word for it.

But, while we can't know *when* the end will come, I believe we can know *what* will happen when the end comes. God has given us a reliable guide, a sure word about the future.

# CAN ANYONE KNOW THE FUTURE?

## The Search for Answers

"It's very difficult to prophesy, especially about the future."

CHINESE PROVERB

World Trade Centers Fall
Market Meltdown...Dow Drops 778 Points
Deadly Flu Pandemic
Middle East Crisis Hits the Boiling Point
Threat of Nuclear 9/11
Doomsday 2012

None of us ever thought we would ever see headlines like these. Yet they have come to flood the news with surreal regularity. The news all around us is gloomy. Security eludes us like a phantom. The foundations of our society seem to be crumbling under our feet. Long-range planning is next to impossible. No one knows what lies ahead, yet everyone wants to know.

One of the most important questions we can ask is, How can we know which scenario of the end times or end of the world is correct? Could the 2012 theory be true? Does the Bible have the answer to what's ahead? Or should we look somewhere else? Is there any way to be certain about what the future holds?

## Put It to the Test

I believe that the only way to know which version of the apocalypse is true is to ask a very simple question: Which view of the future has a proven track record we can examine? Which apocalypse has the "ring of truth"?

The answer for me is clear: only the Bible. The Bible is the best place—the *only* place—to look for ultimate answers. Even the most skeptical person can put the prophecies of the Bible to the test by noting the literal, precise fulfillment of past prophecies. In fact, the God of the Bible is so certain that only He can accurately predict the future that He throws down the gauntlet and challenges any other so-called god to tell the future:

> Remember this, and be assured; recall it to mind, you transgressors. Remember the former things long past, for I am God, and there is no other; I am God, and there is no one like Me, declaring the end from the beginning, and from ancient times things which have not been done, saying, "My purpose will be established, and I will accomplish all My good pleasure"...Truly I have spoken; truly I will bring it to pass. I have planned it, surely I will do it (Isaiah 46:9-11).

In order to accurately predict the future, one must be omniscient (know everything), omnipresent (be present everywhere), and omnipotent (possess all power). The true prognosticator must know all things, must be present at all times and places, and must possess all power so as to make sure the prediction is fulfilled. Only the true God meets these prerequisites, so only He can accurately forecast the future. He is infinite; every other being is finite. And He has proven His ability to tell the future by compiling a 100 percent track record. God bats a perfect one thousand when it comes to predicting the future.

Again, the Bible is the best place—really, the only place— to look for sure answers about the future. Bible prophecy is the lens through which we can look to view the events and issues in today's headlines. I'm not alone in this belief. According to surveys, most Americans believe that the Bible holds the key to this world's future. Here are a few statistics that reveal what Americans believe about the book of Revelation and the end times:

- 59 percent believe the prophecies in Revelation will come true

- Nearly 25 percent believe that the Bible predicted the 9/11 attack

- 35 percent are paying more attention to how news events might relate to the end of the world and Bible prophecy[1]

As we saw in Isaiah 46:9-11, the God of the Bible has issued a challenge to any would-be rivals to His place of supremacy in the universe. The basis of the challenge is that only the true God can accurately predict the future. Let's read what God says about His unique ability to forecast the future.

### Isaiah 41:21-24

"Present your case," the Lord says. "Bring forward your strong arguments," the King of Jacob says. Let them bring forth and declare to us what is going to take place; as the former events, declare what they were, that we may consider them and know their outcome. Or announce to us what is coming; declare the things that are going to come afterward, that we may know that you are gods; indeed, do good or evil, that we may anxiously look about us and fear together. Behold, you are of no account, and your work amounts to nothing; he who chooses you is an abomination.

### Isaiah 42:9

Behold, the former things have come to pass, now I declare new things; before they spring forth I proclaim them to you.

### Isaiah 44:6-8

Thus says the LORD, the King of Israel and his Redeemer, the LORD of hosts: "I am the first and I am the last, and there is no God besides Me."

### Daniel 2:20-22

Let the name of God be blessed forever and ever, for wisdom and power belong to Him. It is he who changes the times and the epochs; He removes kings and establishes kings; He gives wisdom to wise men and knowledge to men of understanding. It is He who reveals the profound and hidden things; He knows what is in the darkness, and the light dwells with Him.

Only the one true God can predict the future, and He can do it with 100 percent accuracy. He has proved it time and time again. All others who claim to be able to predict the future are flimsy, fallible imposters of the one true God.

The biblical prophets didn't speak in vague generalities like Nostradamus and other so-called prophets. If one reads the "prophecies" of Nostradamus with any degree of objectivity, it quickly becomes clear that his prognostications could apply to hundreds of events. His alleged prophecies are discernible only in hindsight and with a great deal of imagination. Supporters of 2012 theories try to point to a few Mayan prophecies that have allegedly come true, but these too are sparse and frequently vague. And even if a few prophecies do come true, that doesn't prove anything. If anyone makes a large enough number of predictions, some of them are bound to come true. Bible prophets, by contrast, gave very specific statements about future events that can easily be checked out and confirmed. They require no fertile imagination or stretching of the limits of credulity.

## Fortune 500

Prophecy expert John Walvoord, in his book *Prophecy Knowledge Handbook,* underscores the astonishing reliability of Bible prophecy. Dr. Walvoord did something that no one else has ever done, as far as I know. He explained every prophecy in the Bible from Genesis to Revelation, which is a tall order. He said this endeavor took him a year and a half. He covered about 1000 prophetic passages, some of which were single verses, and others of which were entire chapters. As a result of his study, he discovered that half of these prophecies, some 500 of them, had already been literally fulfilled. What are the mathematical probabilities of that? The number is too large to comprehend. Walvoord concluded: "We have solid intellectual history that tells us that when God predicts something, it's going to come about."[2] No other prophet or book can even come close to the Bible's record.

## The Voice of the Prophets

Most people are probably unaware that 28 percent of the Bible was prophetic at the time it was written. The Old Testament books record the lives and works of many great prophets—Moses, Isaiah, Jeremiah, Ezekiel, Daniel, Hosea, Joel, Micah, and others. These men predicted future events in vivid detail, including the rise and fall of every major world empire that left its mark on the Middle East. Some of their predictions came true within their lifetimes. And today, it appears that the stage is being set for many others of their astounding prophecies to be fulfilled at any time.

Moving on to the New Testament, Jesus Himself claimed to be a prophet and quoted from Moses, Isaiah, Daniel, and Jeremiah—many times adding interpretive comments and detailed predictions of His own. His words have been confirmed by the test of time. In fact, Jesus' prediction of the fall of Jerusalem (Luke 21:20-24) was so graphic that the early church in Jerusalem was able to escape almost certain destruction by fleeing the city before the Roman general Titus destroyed it in A.D. 70.

Jesus predicted the persecution of the church, the fall of Jerusalem, the destruction of the temple, the scattering of the Jews to all nations, and the amazing survival and growth of the church. Along with the Old Testament prophets, He saw a time when Israel would be reestablished as a nation (Matthew 19:28; Acts 1:6-7). All this has been realized in history. But He also warned those who understood the Old Testament prophets to watch Jerusalem and the Middle East for signs of the approaching end of world civilization, the end of the age of the Gentiles, also referred to in some Bible translations as the times of the Gentiles. The Jews, He said "will fall by the edge of the sword, and will be led captive into all the nations; and Jerusalem will be trampled underfoot by the Gentiles until the times of the Gentiles are fulfilled" (Luke 21:24).

Over five million Jews are now back in the land today. The twentieth century saw the largest return of Jews in history—far more than the two million who left Egypt for the Promised Land under Moses. For the first time since A.D. 135, there are now more Jews living in Israel than in any other place on earth. Jerusalem, the city of dispute and negotiation, was won in 1967, only to become the object of a diplomatic tug-of-war as the prophet Zechariah predicted in about 520 B.C. (Zechariah 12:1-3).

So that you can see for yourself just how specific biblical prophecy is, consider this list, which is far from exhaustive, of some of the prophecies that have already been fulfilled precisely as predicted.

| 10 Fulfilled Biblical Prophecies | | |
|---|---|---|
| Prophecy | Written or Stated | Fulfilled |
| *Genesis 49:10* Messiah will be from the tribe of Judah | ca. 1440 B.C. | 5 B.C. |
| *Isaiah 53* The death of the Messiah | ca. 700 B.C. | A.D. 33 |
| *Daniel 2 and 7* Four Gentile world empires (Babylon, Medo-Persia, Greece, Rome, and a reunited Roman Empire) | ca. 530 B.C. | Throughout history beginning in 605 B.C.— to be continued in the end times. |
| *Daniel 9:24-26* 483 years after a decree to restore and rebuild Jerusalem, Messiah the Prince will come (173,880 days from March 5, 444 B.C. to March 30, A.D. 33, fulfilled to the very day) | ca. 530 B.C. | March 30, A.D. 33 The triumphal entry |

| | | |
|---|---|---|
| *Micah 5:2*<br>Messiah born in Bethlehem | ca. 700 B.C. | 5 B.C. |
| *Isaiah 40:3*<br>Messiah preceded by a<br>messenger | ca. 700 B.C. | A.D. 30<br>John the Baptist |
| *Zechariah 9:9*<br>Messiah will enter Jerusalem<br>riding on a donkey | ca. 520 B.C. | A.D. 33<br>The triumphal entry |
| *Matthew 24:1-3*<br>Jesus prophesied the second<br>Jewish temple would be<br>destroyed | A.D. 33 | A.D. 70 |
| *Matthew 24:9,14*<br>Jesus prophesied that His<br>following would grow into a<br>worldwide movement that<br>would experience persecution | A.D. 33 | Throughout the cur-<br>rent age |

What are the odds of even one of these prophecies being fulfilled perfectly? And these are just ten of the hundreds of biblical prophecies that could be cited. Experts claim that there are about 300 Old Testament prophecies that were fulfilled just in the first coming of Christ. Thirty-three specific prophecies were fulfilled just in the final 24 hours of Jesus' life on earth.[3] The odds of one person coincidentally fulfilling just eight of these prophecies, in an entire lifetime, is 10 to the 17th power. That's a 10 with 17 zeros after it.

Since a number that large is difficult for us to imagine, consider this simple illustration. Suppose you were to spread silver dollars two feet deep across the whole state of Texas. Then you mark just one of them, and bury it somewhere in the state. The chances of a blindfolded person picking up that marked silver dollar on his first try would be one in 10 to the 17th power.[4] And that's just eight prophecies about Jesus! If we added in the hundreds of fulfilled prophecies, the number would defy comprehension.

## Case Closed

Needless to say, the Bible has an unparalleled, unrivaled track record. No other book or prophet even comes close. And no other book or prophet even *claims* to come close. The Bible has the fingerprint or handwriting of God upon it. Fulfilled prophecy proves the veracity and reliability of the Bible. It proves that Jesus Christ is who He claimed to be—the Son of God, God in human flesh. It also proves that the prophecies in the Bible that have yet to be fulfilled will be fulfilled just as literally and exactly as the ones that have already come to pass.

So, what does the Bible say will happen in the last days? What's out there beyond the headlights?

9

# FUTURE TENSE

## What on Earth Is Going to Happen?

"The whole world is sighing and suffering on a scale perhaps
not known in human history: the refugees, the starving...
the terrorism and hostages, the wars, and a thousand other
troubles which beset every country in the world. There are
no people anywhere that are immune. The rich and famous
suffer as well as the poor and obscure...It seems that the
human race may well be heading toward the climax of the
tears, hurts and wounds of the centuries—Armageddon!"

BILLY GRAHAM, *TILL ARMAGEDDON*

From 1996–2000 there was a popular program on television
named *Early Edition*. The plot outline of the show was quite
simple. The main character, Gary Hobson, received the next day's
newspaper a day early. He received tomorrow's newspaper today.
He didn't know how; he didn't know why. All he knew was that
from the time the early edition hit his doorstep, he had 24 hours
to act to prevent terrible things from happening.

When you think about it, God's prophetic word in the Bible
is our "early edition" of future events. It's like having tomorrow's

newspaper today. Someone has wisely said, "If you want to know what happened yesterday, read the newspaper; if you want to know what happened today, listen to the evening news; if you want to know what will happen tomorrow, read the Bible." While this early edition doesn't tell us everything or answer all our questions, it does provide us with the headlines of the future. I believe you'll be amazed at what this early edition says about the future and how events in our world today bear an amazing correspondence to what the Bible says. Let's do a big-picture flyover of the panorama of prophecy.

## The Rapture Shocks the World

According to the Bible, the next great event on God's prophetic calendar could happen any day. The world will be traumatized by the fulfillment of what theologians call the rapture of the church—the sudden removal of every Christian from the world. This will fulfill a promise Jesus gave to His disciples: "Do not let your heart be troubled; believe in God, believe also in Me. In My Father's house are many dwelling places; if it were not so, I would have told you; for I go to prepare a place for you. If I go and prepare a place for you, I will come again and receive you to Myself, that where I am, there you may be also" (John 14:1-3). When the rapture occurs, Christians who have died will be resurrected, and every Christian alive on the earth at that time will be suddenly removed to heaven without experiencing death.

While the rapture is referred to multiple times in the New Testament, there are two main passages that describe the rapture of the church in detail. Carefully reading each of these passages will help you get a basic overview of what this event is about.

Now I say this, brethren, that flesh and blood cannot inherit the kingdom of God; nor does the perishable inherit the imperishable. Behold, I tell you a mystery; we will not all sleep, but we will all be changed, in a moment, in the twinkling of an eye, at the last trumpet; for the trumpet will sound, and the dead will be raised imperishable, and we will be changed. For this perishable must put on the imperishable, and this mortal must put on immortality. But when this perishable will have put on the imperishable, and this mortal will have put on immortality, then will come about the saying that is written, "Death is swallowed up in victory. O death, where is your victory? O death, where is your sting?" The sting of death is sin, and the power of sin is the law; but thanks be to God, who gives us the victory through our Lord Jesus Christ (1 Corinthians 15:50-57).

We do not want you to be uninformed, brethren, about those who are asleep, so that you will not grieve as do the rest who have no hope. For if we believe that Jesus died and rose again, even so God will bring with Him those who have fallen asleep in Jesus. For this we say to you by the word of the Lord, that we who are alive and remain until the coming of the Lord, will not precede those who have fallen asleep. For the Lord Himself will descend from heaven with a shout, with the voice of the archangel and with the trumpet of God, and the dead in Christ will rise first. Then we who are alive and remain will be caught up together with them in the clouds to meet the Lord in the air, and so we shall always be with the Lord. Therefore comfort one another with these words (1 Thessalonians 4:13-18).

When the rapture occurs, every living believer in Jesus Christ will be snatched off planet earth and whisked away to heaven in the amount of time it takes to blink your eye. It will be the most world-changing event since the flood that covered the earth in the days of Noah. The rapture will change everything. Think of the mass chaos and confusion that will result. The disappearance of millions of Christians will deepen the religious confusion that is rampant today and is evident in the current cultural obsession over the supernatural and mystical phenomena (as is the case in the New Age movement). With every true Christian removed, the organized church will quickly fall into the hands of self-seeking opportunists.

Think about this for a moment: The major difference between the Christian hope of the rapture and the scenario predicted in 2012 is that believers in Jesus Christ are waiting for a person, not destruction. To the Christian, the rapture is a blessed hope (Titus 2:13). It's a comfort in the midst of this turbulent world we live in.

Interestingly, José Arguelles, a key figure in the 2012 movement, is also expecting a mass disappearance of people from the earth. He maintains that those who have not evolved enough spiritually will disappear from the earth someday—maybe soon. Arguelles has recently moved to New Zealand to await the great transition. He claims that in 1993, he received a prophecy in Hawaii and since that time he has called himself Valum Votan, "Closer of the Cycle." Arguelles says, "The post-2012 world will be a world of universal telepathy. We'll literally be living in a new time...There will be a lot fewer of us, with simple lifestyles, solar technology, garden culture and lots of telepathic communication."[1] Then he makes this startling statement about those who "have not evolved spiritually enough to know that there are other dimensions of reality." Arguelles predicts that they will be taken away from earth in "silver ships."[2] This sounds a lot like the rapture predicted in the

Bible. Millions of people will disappear from the earth. This may be one of the ways those who are left behind at the rapture will try to explain away the disappearance of millions of people. They will tell the world that those who disappeared were not spiritually evolved enough. This kind of New Age spiritual deception will pave the way for increasing delusion during the Tribulation, which will result in the world accepting the Antichrist as God (2 Thessalonians 2:11).

The poster for the movie *2012* is black and ominous with "2012" in large letters in the middle. Across the top of the poster are the words, "Who will be left behind?" This appears to be another tie-in with the rapture theology of the Bible. Is this seeming reference to the rapture on purpose? Could it be an intentional allusion to the popular Left Behind® series of novels authored by Tim LaHaye and Jerry Jenkins? I don't know for sure, but it's interesting that New Age eschatology makes reference to people being left behind. In their scenario, being left behind is evidently a good thing because it means you survived the 2012 cataclysm. By contrast, from a biblical perspective, being left behind at the rapture is a tragic thing. Could the New Age view be a subtle attempt by New Agers to make people feel secure and positive about being left behind at the rapture?

## The Seven-year Tribulation

As we have already seen, the Bible strictly forbids attempting to determine the specific date for end-time events. However, there *is* one prophecy in the Bible that mentions a specific time. We find it in Daniel 9:24-27, one of the most important prophetic sections in the Bible. It is the indispensable key to all prophecy. It has often been called the "Backbone of Bible Prophecy," and

"God's Prophetic Time Clock." This prophecy tells us that God has put Israel's future on a time clock.

The setting for this prophecy is found in Daniel 9:1-23. The prophet Daniel is in Babylon, where the Jewish people have been in exile for almost 70 years. Daniel knows from reading the prophecies of Jeremiah that the captivity will last only 70 years. In Daniel 9:1-23, Daniel confesses the sins of the Jewish people and prays about the restoration of the people from Babylon. He knows that the 70 years of captivity is over (9:1-2), so he begins to intercede for his people. While Daniel is praying, God sends an immediate answer by the angel Gabriel (9:21). Daniel 9:24-27 is God's answer to Daniel's prayer, and in this answer, God goes far beyond the restoration of the people from Babylon. He goes all the way to Israel's ultimate and final restoration under Messiah.

> Seventy weeks have been decreed for your people and your holy city, to finish the transgression, to make an end of sin, to make atonement for iniquity, to bring in everlasting righteousness, to seal up vision and prophecy and to anoint the most holy place. So you are to know and discern that from the issuing of a decree to restore and rebuild Jerusalem until Messiah the Prince there will be seven weeks and sixty-two weeks; it will be built again, with plaza and moat, even in times of distress. Then after the sixty-two weeks the Messiah will be cut off and have nothing, and the people of the prince who is to come will destroy the city and the sanctuary. And its end will come with a flood; even to the end there will be war; desolations are determined. And he will make a firm covenant with the many for one week, but in the middle of this week he will put a stop to sacrifice and grain offering; and on the wing of abominations will come one who makes desolate, even until a complete destruction,

one that is decreed, is poured out on the one who makes desolate (Daniel 9:24-27).

Bible scholars generally interpret each week as a period of seven years because Daniel had already been thinking in terms of years in Daniel 9:1-2. The entire period involved, therefore, is 490 years (70 sets of 7-year periods using a 360-day prophetic year). The prophecy goes on to predict that 7 of these sevens (49 years) will pass while Jerusalem is rebuilt and 62 more sevens (434 years) will transpire until the Messiah comes as Israel's prince. The total of the first 69 sevens is 483 years (49 + 434 is 483 years). Using simple calculation, we can determine that the divine prophetic clock began ticking on March 5, 444 B.C., when the Persian king Artaxerxes issued a decree allowing the Jews to return under Nehemiah's leadership to rebuild the city of Jerusalem (Nehemiah 1).

From the time the countdown began until the coming of Messiah ("the Anointed One") will be 69 weeks (7 weeks + 62 weeks), or 483 years. This exact period of time, which is 173,880 days when using the Jewish calendar of 360 days for a year, is the precise number of days that elapsed from March 5, 444 B.C. until March 30, A.D. 33, the day that Jesus rode into Jerusalem for the triumphal entry.[3] I often say that this is the greatest prophecy in the Bible. God predicted a period of 173,880 days to the exact day!

As you can see, this leaves one "seven" or "week" still left for the future. God's prophetic clock for Israel stopped at the end of week 69. We are presently living in this period of unspecified duration between weeks 69 and 70, which is called the church age. The church age will end when Christ comes to rapture His bride, the church, to heaven. God's prophetic clock for Israel will begin to run again, after the church has been raptured to heaven, when the Antichrist comes onto the scene and makes a seven-year peace treaty with Israel (Daniel 9:27). This is the final or seventieth "seven" that still remains to be fulfilled. It's often referred to as the seventieth week of Daniel.

In the middle of the final seven-year period of this age, the end-time world ruler, the Antichrist, will break his treaty with Israel, turn against the Jews, and desecrate a rebuilt temple in Jerusalem. This act of desecration prophesied by Daniel, called the abomination of desolation, was also prophesied by Jesus 500 years after Daniel as He looked down the corridor of time to the end of days (Matthew 24:15). The abomination of desolation will begin with the Antichrist defiling the temple by sitting in its holy of holies and declaring himself God (2 Thessalonians 2:4). He will then have an image of himself constructed that will sit in the temple, and all will be forced to worship him and the image (Revelation 13:14-18). At the culmination of the final seven-year period, the Antichrist will be destroyed by Christ at His second coming to earth.

| Overview of the 70 Weeks (Daniel 9:24-27) | |
|---|---|
| Daniel 9:24 | The entire 70 weeks (490 years) |
| Daniel 9:25 | The first 69 weeks, or 7 weeks + 62 weeks (483 years) |
| Daniel 9:26 | The time between week 69 and week 70 (? years, the current age) |
| Daniel 9:27 | Week 70 (7 years) |

How does all this relate to 2012? I believe the 70-weeks prophecy of Daniel is one of the key clues we have that demonstrates that 2012 will not be the time of the second coming of Christ or

## Daniel's Seventy Weeks
### (Daniel 9:24-27)

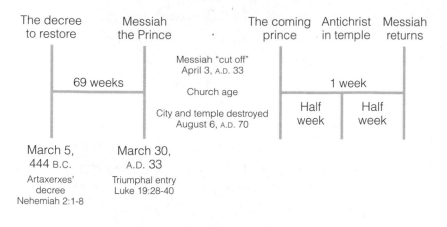

the end of the world. According to Daniel, the second coming of Christ will be preceded by a seven-year period that Jesus called the Tribulation.

If 2012 were the end of this age, then based on Daniel's prophecy, we would have to back up at least seven years to 2005, which would be the beginning of Daniel's seventieth week. That means the rapture would have to have already happened, and the Tribulation would have had to start in 2005. While we have witnessed many unique tragedies in our world during the last few years, I think almost everyone would agree that the rapture hasn't occurred and the seven-year Tribulation period Daniel predicted has not started yet. For me, God's end time-clock in Daniel 9:24-27 settles the issue once for all: 2012 will not be doomsday.

With this understanding of God's time clock, especially as it relates to 2012, let's get back to our overview of God's end-time template—the panorama of prophecy.

## Power Centralized in One Man

After the rapture, as you can imagine, the world will be searching for answers. From the many negotiators and leaders jockeying for position will come one new international leader who will emerge from Europe to superimpose a peace settlement between Israel and its militant Muslim neighbors to solve the Middle East crisis and possibly also to assure the West's supply of oil. This will bring an era of false peace, a move toward disarmament, and a major push for a new world economic system. The early part of the coming Tribulation will be the calm before the storm as the new leader consolidates his power. But it won't be long before trouble begins to break out and difficulties begin to mount.

The last three-and-a-half years of this seven-year period will include a series of almost inconceivable catastrophes. Just before this period begins, Russia and a group of Islamic allies will attempt a final bid for power in the Middle East, but their armies will be supernaturally destroyed (Ezekiel 38–39). The balance of power will swing decisively to the world's new strongman, the Antichrist. As Satan's man of the hour, the Antichrist will then attempt to destroy Israel, now disarmed and at peace. In the fashion of the Babylonian and Roman emperors, he will deify himself and command the worship of the world.

## A Series of Natural Disasters

During the Tribulation, the world will come apart at the seams. Disasters will occur on a scale worse than that found in any ecologist's nightmare. Jesus told His disciples about this time and the devastation that would occur. The setting was Jesus' farewell message shortly before His crucifixion. Jesus had been with the disciples for more than three years, and they still did not understand what was about to happen to their leader. Two days later, on Friday, He would be nailed to a Roman cross and suffer a cruel, barbaric death. But while it was still Wednesday of the final week of His life, as He was accompanied by His disciples on a hill east of Jerusalem called the Mount of Olives, Jesus unveiled for them a sweeping panorama of the future.

Jesus and the Twelve slowly ascended the summit of the hill that overlooked the Temple Mount 200 feet below. It was Passover season, so the temple precinct would have been teeming with pilgrims. When they reached the summit, Jesus seated Himself on a rock, and four of the disciples, Peter, James, John, and Andrew, approached Him privately and asked a penetrating question that had probably been burning in their hearts for some time: "Tell us, when will these things happen, and what will be the sign of Your coming, and of the end of the age?" (Matthew 24:3; see also Mark 13:3). As the late afternoon shadows lengthened over the city of Jerusalem, Israel's premiere prophet began to paint a gloomy portrait of the end of the age. He told His followers that the worst was yet to come.

One point comes through loud and clear in Jesus' answer to His disciples: This world is not going to become a better place to live in. Times of almost unbelievable difficulty are on the horizon. Jesus said that the end of the age will be a unique time of terror. Nothing in all of world history will compare to what is coming. It will totally eclipse all previous history in terms of hardship and trouble. "There will be a great tribulation, such as has not occurred since the beginning of the world until now, nor ever will" (Matthew 24:21).

Now that's saying a lot, because there have been some terrible times in the past, haven't there? Plagues that wiped out millions. Widespread famines. World wars. Massive earthquakes.

The Holocaust. During the Tribulation, the terror and destruction will be nationwide and worldwide in scope, and it will be worse than anything that has happened before. There will be disasters of unimaginable horror and magnitude.

Acts of man, resulting in thousands of martyrs, and acts of God, will combine to cause great disturbances in the world and solar system. Stars will fall and planets will run off course, causing chaotic changes in climate (Revelation 16:8-9,13-14). Unnatural heat and cold, flooding, and other disasters will wipe out much of the food production of the world (Revelation 6:6-8). Great famines will cause millions to perish (Matthew 24:7). Strange new pandemics will sweep the world, killing millions (Revelation 6:6-8). As the period draws to a close, earthquakes will level the great cities of the world, and geographic upheavals will cause mountains and islands to disappear in the seas (Revelation 16:17-20). In the course of just a few years, disaster after disaster will reduce the world population to a fraction of its present billions.

Revelation 6–19 is the main passage in the Bible that describes the Tribulation. These 14 chapters give an overview of the terrible judgments of the end times. These chapters tell us that God will pour out three sets of seven judgments upon the earth.

There are seven seal judgments (Revelation 6), seven trumpet judgments (Revelation 8–9), and seven bowl judgments (Revelation 16). These series of judgments will be poured out successively during the Tribulation.

7 Seals ⟶ 7 Trumpets ⟶ 7 Bowls

The seven seals will be opened during the first half of the Tribulation. The seven trumpets will be blown during the second half of the Tribulation. And the seven bowls will be poured out during a very brief period of time right near the end of the Tribulation, just before Christ returns.

| First Half of Tribulation | Second Half of Tribulation | Second Coming |
|---|---|---|
| 7 Seals | 7 Trumpets | 7 Bowls |

In Scripture, these judgments are frequently compared to birth pangs (Jeremiah 30:4-7; Matthew 24:8; 1 Thessalonians 5:3). As the Tribulation progresses, as is the case with birth pangs, these judgments will irreversibly intensify in their severity and frequency.

These three successive crashing waves of God's judgment are described in detail in Revelation 6–19.

### Seven Seal Judgments

First Seal (6:1-2)—white horse: Antichrist

Second Seal (6:3-4)—red horse: war

Third Seal (6:5-6)—black horse: famine

Fourth Seal (6:7-8)—pale horse: death and hell

Fifth Seal (6:9-11)—martyrs in heaven

Sixth Seal (6:12-17)—universal upheaval and devastation

Seventh Seal (8:1-2)—the seven trumpets

### Seven Trumpet Judgments

First Trumpet (8:7)—bloody hail and fire: one-third of vegetation destroyed

Second Trumpet (8:8-9)—fireball from heaven: one-third of oceans polluted

Third Trumpet (8:10-11)—falling star: one-third of fresh water polluted

Fourth Trumpet (8:12)—darkness: one-third of sun, moon and stars darkened

Fifth Trumpet (9:1-12)—demonic invasion: torment

Sixth Trumpet (9:13-21)—demonic army: one-third of mankind killed

Seventh Trumpet (11:15-19)—the kingdom: the announcement of Christ's reign

## Seven Bowl Judgments

First Bowl (16:2)—upon the earth: sores on the worshipers of the Antichrist

Second Bowl (16:3)—upon the seas: turned to blood

Third Bowl (16:4-7)—upon the fresh water: turned to blood

Fourth Bowl (16:8-9)—upon the sun: intense, scorching heat

Fifth Bowl (16:10-11)—upon the Antichrist's kingdom: darkness and pain

Sixth Bowl (16:12-16)—upon the Euphrates River: Armageddon

Seventh Bowl (16:17-21)—upon the air: earthquakes and hail

It boggles the mind just to read this list. One-half of the earth's population will perish in just two of the 19 judgments (Revelation

6:8; 9:18). The environment of the entire planet will be destroyed. Revelation 16:19-21 graphically pictures the worldwide devastation: "The cities of the nations fell…And every island fled away, and the mountains were not found. And huge hailstones, about one hundred pounds each, came down from heaven upon men."

Just imagine living on earth while all that is transpiring.

## The March to Armageddon

Topping even these disasters will be a world war of unprecedented proportions. Hundreds of millions of people will be involved in a gigantic, global power struggle centered in the Holy Land (Revelation 16:13-16). The area will become the scene of the greatest war of history. Great armies from every nation will pour into the Middle East for earth's final death struggle (Zechariah 12:1-3). Climaxing the struggle will be millions of men from the East, probably including China, who will cross the Euphrates River and join the fray (Revelation 16:12). Millions will perish in this deadly struggle known as Armageddon.

Armageddon, in our culture, has come to describe anyone's worst fear of the end of the world, but the biblical prophets have described it more specifically as the final war of a desperate world struggle centered in the Middle East. It will be the final act in a terrifying series of events that are very much related to today's headlines. This history-shattering war will occur (1) on schedule, (2) at a specific time, and (3) in its predicted location. The name *Armageddon* comes from a Hebrew word meaning "the Mount of Megiddo," which is a small mountain located in northern Israel at the end of a broad valley. This valley has been the scene of many military conflicts in the past and will be the focal point of this great future conflict.

Before this mother of all wars is resolved and the victor determined, Jesus Christ will come back in power and glory from heaven. He will be accompanied by millions of angels and raptured Christians, and His coming is described in graphic terms in Revelation 19:11-16.

> I saw heaven opened; and behold, a white horse, and He who sat on it is called Faithful and True, and in righteousness He judges and wages war. His eyes are a flame of fire, and on His head are many diadems; and He has a name written on Him which no one knows except Himself. He is clothed with a robe dipped in blood, and His name is called The Word of God. And the armies which are in heaven, clothed in fine linen, white and clean, were following Him on white horses. From His mouth comes a sharp sword, so that with it He may strike down the nations, and He will rule them with a rod of iron; and He treads the wine press of the fierce wrath of God, the Almighty. And on His robe and on His thigh He has a name written, "King of kings, and Lord of lords."

Coming as the King of kings and judge of the world, Jesus will destroy the contending armies and bring in His own kingdom of peace and righteousness on earth. As incredible as these prophecies are, even now the world stage is being set. The nations are taking their predicted places. Ancient prophecies will be fulfilled. The world will rush to Armageddon!

## There's a New World Coming

Man has always dreamed of a utopia, a great society, a paradise on earth, a return to the Garden of Eden—paradise regained. This is the grand vision for many 2012 disciples. And they are partially correct. The Bible does predict that a new world is coming, a really new world order. The Bible says that this present world will undergo a great purification process and that there will be a global transformation in consciousness. Yet the Bible is clear that man can never produce such a society on earth in his own strength and ingenuity. The new chapter in human history won't come because of some harmonic convergence or quantum leap in human awareness. It will follow the time of great tribulation when Jesus returns to this earth in power and great glory, The second coming of Jesus Christ will usher in a period of time commonly referred to as the millennial kingdom or the 1000-year reign of Jesus on earth as King of kings and Lord of lords (*mille* in Latin means 1000).

Even 2012 gurus such as Gregg Braden are aware of this. "So what does all this mean for 2012? Are we headed into a time of catastrophe or 1,000 years of peace? Are we looking at Armageddon, Eden, or possibly both?"[4] Braden's comment is interesting because it shows that he has at least some knowledge of the biblical teaching of 1000 years of peace.

Immediately following the return of Christ and the destruction of Antichrist and his armies in Revelation 19:11-21 comes the binding of Satan and the reign of Christ for 1000 years (Revelation 20:1-6). Notice that the words "thousand years" appear six times in Revelation 20:1-7. I believe this 1000-year period refers to a future, literal 1000 years, not some symbolic, extended period of time during this present age.[5] It will be a time when God's original plan for mankind will be fulfilled on earth.

### Key Passages on the Millennium

While Revelation 20:1-6 is the only passage in the Bible that records the length of Christ's reign on the earth, it is not the only passage to refer to His kingdom. The Old Testament is filled with large sections of text on the millennial kingdom. Numerous students of Bible prophecy have noted that there is more prophetic material devoted to the subject of the millennium than to any other single topic. Therefore, it is critical that we gain at least a basic understanding about the millennial kingdom.

For starters, here is a list of ten of the most important Old Testament passages about the coming kingdom. You might take time right now to read them:

1. Isaiah 2:1-5
2. Isaiah 11:1-16
3. Isaiah 32:1-20
4. Isaiah 35:1-10
5. Isaiah 60:1-22
6. Jeremiah 31:1-40
7. Jeremiah 33:1-26
8. Ezekiel 37:14-28
9. Amos 9:11-15
10. Zechariah 14:6-21

### The Real New World Order—Paradise Regained

During the millennial reign of Christ, the earth will experience a return to conditions like those in the Garden of Eden. It will literally be heaven on earth as the Lord of heaven comes to live on the earth among His people. It will be a time of great enlightenment and transformation of global consciousness, but not in the New Age sense. The whole earth will be filled with the knowledge and worship of the true God.

The Bible has a lot more to say about the coming millennium

than most people realize. Here is a list of the ten most prominent conditions that will prevail on the earth during the reign of Christ:

1. *Peace*—All wars will cease as the world is unified under the reign of the true King (Isaiah 2:4; 9:4-7; 11:6-9; Zechariah 9:10).

2. *Joy*—When Isaac Watts wrote the song "Joy to the World," he did not write it to be a Christmas carol. Rather, this song was penned to announce the glorious second coming of Christ to rule and reign on this earth. Consider some of the words of this song: "Joy to the world! The Lord is come; let earth receive her king…No more let sins and sorrows grow…He rules the world with truth and grace." This is a song about the millennium, when true joy will come to the world (Isaiah 9:3-4; 12:3-6; 14:7-8; 25:8-9; 30:29; 42:1; Jeremiah 30:18-19; Zephaniah 3:14-17; Zechariah 8:18-23; 10:6-7).

3. *Holiness*—The word *holy* means to be "set apart" to God for sacred purposes. The kingdom of Christ will be a holy kingdom. Everything in it will be set apart to God for His use. The holiness of the Lord will be manifest in His own person as well as the citizens of His kingdom. The land, the city, the temple, and the subjects will all be holy unto the Lord (Isaiah 4:3-4; 29:19; 35:8; 52:1; Ezekiel 43:7-12; 45:1; Zechariah 8:3; 14:20-21).

4. *Glory*—The radiant glory of God will be fully manifest in Messiah's kingdom (Isaiah 35:2; 40:5; 60:1-9; Ezekiel 43:1-5).

5. *Justice or Righteousness*—When the millennial kingdom

begins, only believers will inhabit it. However, some of these believers (who will have survived the Tribulation and were not raptured) will still have human bodies with a fallen nature capable of sinning. Man's sin will be judged by the administration of perfect justice at the hands of the Messiah (Isaiah 9:7; 11:5; 32:16; 42:1-4; 65:21-23). He will rule with "a rod of iron" (Revelation 2:27), restraining and judging sin so that righteousness will prevail (Isaiah 11:1-5; 60:21; Jeremiah 31:23; Ezekiel 37:23-24; Zephaniah 3:1,13).

6. *Full Knowledge*—The teaching ministry of the Lord and the indwelling Spirit will bring the subjects of the kingdom into a full knowledge of the Lord's ways (Isaiah 11:1-2,9; 41:19-20; 54:13; Jeremiah 31:33-34; Habakkuk 2:14).

7. *Absence of Sickness or Deformity*—Politicians constantly promise to give their citizens better health care. In the Lord's government, the health plan will be out of this world. The King will be both a ruler and a healer who cures all the diseases and deformities of His people (Isaiah 29:18; 33:24; 35:5-6; 61:1-2; Ezekiel 34:16). As a result of this health care plan, people will live extended life spans like those in the time before the worldwide flood. A person who dies at the age of 100 will be considered to have died very prematurely (Isaiah 65:20).

8. *Universal Worship of God*—All the inhabitants of the earth will join their hearts and voices in praise and worship to God and His Christ (Isaiah 45:23; 52:1,7-10; 66:17-23; Zephaniah 3:9; Zechariah 13:2; 14:16; Malachi 1:11; Revelation 5:9-14).

9. *Economic Prosperity*—There won't be any need for

rescue missions, welfare programs, food stamps, government bailouts, or relief agencies in the coming kingdom. The world will flourish under the hand of the King of heaven (Isaiah 35:1-2,7; 30:23-25; 62:8-9; 65:21-23; Jeremiah 31:5,12; Ezekiel 34:26; 36:29-30; Joel 2:21-27; Amos 9:13-14; Micah 4:1,4; Zechariah. 8:11-12; 9:16-17).

10. *The Presence of God*—The greatest thing about the kingdom is that Christ Himself will be there. God's presence will be fully recognized and the Lord's people will experience fellowship with the Lord unlike anything they have ever known (Ezekiel 37:27-28; Zechariah 2:10-13). The city of Jerusalem will be called *Yahweh Shammah,* which means "the Lord is there" (Ezekiel 48:35).

## Seven Key Titles of the Millennium

The title for an event helps shed light on its nature. A title summarizes in a word or brief phrase the essence of an event. For instance, the annual NFL championship game is titled the Super Bowl. The day the allies invaded the beaches of Normandy is called D-day. The day the stock market crashed in 1929 is forever remembered as Black Monday.

Below are some key biblical titles God has given to us to capture the essence of the coming kingdom:

1. the kingdom of heaven (Matthew 3:2; 8:11)

2. the kingdom of God (Mark 1:14)

3. the kingdom (Matthew 19:28)

4. the world to come (Hebrews 2:5)

5. times of refreshing (Acts 3:19)

6. the period of restoration of all things (Acts 3:21)

7. a kingdom that cannot be shaken (Hebrews 12:28)

## Counterfeiting the Truth

As we considered the key events of the end-time scenario presented in the Bible, you may have noticed there are striking parallels between some of the 2012 prophecies and the biblical prophecies. Many ancient predictions do mirror the Bible. Scripture predicts that there will be a time of great trouble and upheaval on the earth that will be climaxed by the second coming of Jesus back to earth. After His coming, Jesus will usher in a 1000-year period of unimaginable utopia on earth. The coming apocalypse in the Bible will be both an end and a beginning—a cataclysm and a rebirth. It will bring an end to injustice, war, strife, hatred, and pollution and will begin an era of universal justice, peace, harmony, joy, and prosperity. This sounds eerily similar to what many people are forecasting for 2012.

It shouldn't surprise us that pagan, New Age prophecies mirror the prophecies of the Bible to some degree because the source of those New Age prophecies are ultimately demonic. We know from the Scriptures that the satanic realm copies and counterfeits God's true prophetic plan of the ages to lead unwary people astray.[6] The New Age eschatology is a corruption of the true biblical template. It is part of the demonically inspired false teaching that the Bible predicted would come in the last days (1 Timothy 4:1). It eliminates God from the scene, eradicates the idea of human sin, and exalts man as His own savior.

Here are some of the striking similarities between the two paradigms as well as some very distinct differences:

| The End Times | |
|---|---|
| **2012 versus the Bible** | |
| **2012** | **The Bible** |
| Unenlightened taken away from earth in "silver ships" | True believers caught up (raptured) to heaven by Christ |
| Future time of great cataclysm called the Shift | Future time of great cataclysm called the Tribulation |
| Global disaster strikes on December 21, 2012 | Global judgment occurs during a seven-year period in the future |
| Caused by galactic alignment | Caused by God's judgment of human sin |
| End of the Mayan calendar | End of the age on God's calendar |
| Followed by a time of heightened global consciousness or harmonic convergence (false utopia) | Followed by Christ's 1000-year reign of peace and righteousness on earth (true utopia) |
| Ultimate goal is for man to reach a higher plane of consciousness—the higher self | Ultimate goal is for God to be glorified |

As you can see, these are two very different scenarios with very different outcomes, goals, and destinies. Be careful which one you choose. Your destiny depends on it. For me, the issue ultimately goes back to which one we can trust. Which one has a proven track record to back it up? Only the Bible has proven 100 percent accurate when it comes to predicting the future.

## The End

In light of all the escalating catastrophes, danger, and uncertainty in our world, more and more people today are asking the ultimate question: When will the world as we know it end? Or will it end?

Let's investigate what the Bible says about this question that more people than ever are asking.

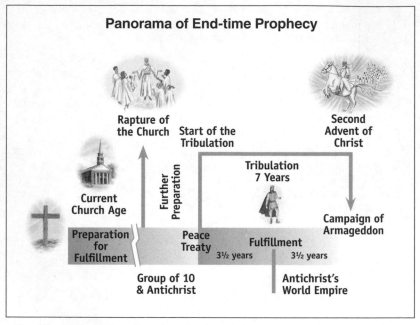

*Here is a visual time line that depicts the sequence of events before and during the Tribulation.*

Adapted and used with permission of Tim LaHaye and Thomas Ice, *Charting the End Times* (Eugene, OR: Harvest House, 2001). The chart above is based on charts that appear in LaHaye and Ice's book, with one adaptation: the placement of the Group of 10 and Antichrist before the signing of the peace treaty rather than after.

## Major Prophecies that Are Yet Unfulfilled

### In Chronological Order

1. Rapture of the church (John 14:1-3; 1 Corinthians 15:51-58; 1 Thessalonians 4:13-18)

2. Reuniting of the Roman Empire under a group of ten leaders— the G-10 (Daniel 7:7,24; Revelation 13:1; 17:3,12-13)

3. Jewish temple rebuilt in Jerusalem (Daniel 9:27; 12:11; Matthew 24:14; 2 Thessalonians 2:4; Revelation 11:1-2)

4. Rise of the Antichrist (Daniel 7:8; Revelation 13:18)

5. Signing of the seven-year peace treaty with Israel (Daniel 9:27)

6. Russia, Iran, and other Islamic allies spring a surprise attack on Israel (Ezekiel 38–39)

7. Peace treaty with Israel broken after three-and-a-half years: beginning of one-world government, one-world economy, and one-world religion (Daniel 7:23; Revelation 13:5-8,15-17; 17:16-17)

8. Mark of the beast established as a pledge of allegiance to the Antichrist and as a passport for doing business (Revelation 13:16-18)

9. Many Christians and Jews martyred for refusing to worship the world dictator and take his mark (Revelation 7:9-17; 13:15)

10. Catastrophic, divine judgments and environmental disasters upon the whole world, represented by seals, trumpets, and bowls (Revelation 6–16)

11. World war breaks out, with the focus on the Middle East—Campaign of Armageddon (Revelation 16:12-16)

12. Babylon destroyed (Revelation 18)

13. Second coming of Christ (Matthew 24:27-31; Revelation 19:11-21)

14. Judgment of unbelievers (Ezekiel 20:33-38; Matthew 25:31-46; Jude 14-15; Revelation 19:15-21; 20:1-4)

15. Satan bound for 1000 years (Revelation 20:1-3)

16. Resurrection of Tribulation saints and Old Testament saints (Daniel 12:2; Revelation 20:4)

17. Millennial (1000 year) kingdom begins (Revelation 20:5-6)

18. Final rebellion at the end of the millennium (Revelation 20:7-10)

19. Resurrection and final judgment of the wicked—Great White Throne Judgment (Revelation 20:11-15)

20. Eternity begins—new heaven, new earth, New Jerusalem (Revelation 21:1-2)[7]

# 10

# IN THE END, GOD

## How Will the World End?

"I saw a new heaven and a new earth;
for the first heaven and the first earth passed away."

REVELATION 21:1

D r. John Walvoord, one of the most recognized authorities on Bible prophecy, told me about an interesting encounter he had while walking through Dallas-Fort Worth International Airport with the editor of *Eternity* magazine. He and the editor were nearing the gate for their flight when a woman who knew Dr. Walvoord approached him and struck up a conversation. Dr. Walvoord introduced the woman to the editor, and she asked, "What do you do?" He responded, "I manage *Eternity.*" To which she replied, "That must be a big job."

Think of what a big job it must be to *really* manage eternity! It boggles the mind just to think about it. But the Bible declares that the all-powerful, transcendent Creator manages every iota of this universe without any effort whatsoever. He is the ruler of all eternity! He is in control of the future, including the end of the world and all that transpires afterward.

Having determined that December 12, 2012 will not mark the end of the world, and that the Bible is the only reliable guide for knowing the future, what does the Bible tell us about how the world will end? While the Bible clearly states the world *will* be destroyed, we are not told certain specifics of how that will come about. Let's consider what we *can* know for sure, based on Scripture.

## Will Earth Be Destroyed by a Nuclear Holocaust?

According to a *Time* magazine poll (October 26, 1998), 51 percent of Americans believe that a man-made disaster will wipe out civilization during the next century. Probably the number one threat people think of is nuclear weapons.

Ever since the dawn of the nuclear age in the 1940s, people have wondered if the world will end in a nuclear nightmare. This fear has been heightened by the recent proliferation of nuclear weapons. Nations such as Pakistan, North Korea, India, and China have nuclear weapons, and it's only a matter of time before rogue states (such as Iran) and terrorist organizations have access to "the bomb."

There are some passages of Scripture that have been used by prophecy teachers to support the idea that the world will be destroyed by nuclear weapons: Isaiah 24:18-20; Zechariah 14:12; and 2 Peter 3:7,10-14. I have personally heard several sermons in which 2 Peter 3:7,10-14 was interpreted as graphically describing a great nuclear explosion that blows up the earth. Zechariah 14:12 describes the flesh of people rotting as they stand on their feet, with their eyes rotting in the sockets and their tongues rotting in their mouths. This is interpreted by some as describing what happens to people who are exposed to a nuclear explosion.

I don't believe the Bible tells us specifically whether nuclear weapons will be used in the destruction of this earth. The Bible passages that some people cite as referring to a nuclear detonation seem to refer to divine judgment directly from the hand of God rather than a nuclear explosion at the hand of humans (Revelation 8:6-12). However one interprets those passages, the Bible clearly states this world will not be destroyed by man or any man-made disaster. The Bible states in Genesis 1:1 that God created the heavens and the earth, and declares in 2 Peter 3:5-7 that God will someday destroy the present heaven and earth with fire.

> When they maintain this, it escapes their notice that by the word of God the heavens existed long ago and the earth was formed out of water and by water, through which the world at that time was destroyed, being flooded with water. But by His word the present heavens and earth are being reserved for fire, kept for the day of judgment and destruction of ungodly men.

So it is God Himself who will "push the button" to destroy this world, not some Middle Eastern madman or galactic alignment. The God who created this world is in total control of His creation. There's not a single maverick molecule in this vast universe. No man will ever destroy this earth. God has reserved this right for Himself.

### The Fire Next Time

In the movie *2012,* the end of the world is marked by convulsing earthquakes, supervolcanic eruptions, and meteorites bombarding the earth. The final blow is a flood of biblical proportions. Waves crash over the Himalayas and floodwaters are shown inundating Washington, D.C. The world ends in a great flood.

Many 2012olgists predict cataclysmic floods that will kill 90 percent of all life on earth. This deluge scenario stands in direct contradiction to the Noahic Covenant in the book of Genesis. The Bible says that after the worldwide flood in Noah's day, God made a unilateral, unconditional, eternal covenant with Noah and the human race never to destroy the earth again by water.

> God spoke to Noah and to his sons with him, saying, "Now behold, I Myself do establish My covenant with you, and with your descendants after you; and with every living creature that is with you, the birds, the cattle, and every beast of the earth with you; of all that comes out of the ark, even every beast of the earth. I establish My covenant with you; and all flesh shall never again be cut off by the water of the flood, neither shall there again be a flood to destroy the earth" (Genesis 9:8-11).

The world will end someday, but not from a great flood. According to the Bible, it will be destroyed by fire: "By His word the present heavens and earth are being reserved for fire, kept for the day of judgment...the heavens will pass away with a roar and the elements will be destroyed with intense heat, and the earth and its works will be burned up" (2 Peter 3:7,10). The same God who created the world by His spoken word in Genesis will one day speak the word that causes the present heavens and earth to come apart in a fiery conflagration. Then He will create a new heavens and new earth (verse 13).

## New Heavens and Earth

According to Scripture, there is more to come after the 1000-year reign of Christ. After the millennium will come what the Bible calls "a new heaven and a new earth" (Revelation 21:1). The promise of a new heaven and new earth are first recorded in the Old Testament by the prophet Isaiah: "For behold, I create new heavens and a new earth; and the former things will not be remembered or come to mind" (Isaiah 65:17). In the very next verse, Isaiah predicts a new Jerusalem and a time with no more tears or pain. Isaiah was privileged to see further in the future than any other Old Testament prophet, and his vision of the future world is amplified by the apostle John in Revelation 21:

> I saw a new heaven and a new earth; for the first heaven and the first earth passed away, and there is no longer any sea. And I saw the holy city, new Jerusalem, coming down out of heaven from God, made ready as a bride adorned for her husband. And I heard a loud voice from the throne, saying, "Behold, the tabernacle of God is among men, and He will dwell among them, and they shall be His people, and God Himself will be among them, and He will wipe away every tear from their eyes; and there will no longer be any death; there will no longer be any mourning, or crying, or pain; the first things have passed away." And He who sits on the throne said, "Behold, I am making all things new." And He said, "Write, for these words are faithful and true." Then He said to me "It is done. I am the Alpha and the Omega, the beginning and the end" (Revelation 21:1-6).

Obviously, for there to be a new heaven and a new earth, something must happen to the present heaven and earth. It must either undergo a complete renovation or be destroyed. Which will it be?

## Renovation or Annihilation?

Many Bible teachers contend that the present heaven and earth will simply be the old earth renovated and restored.[1] I agree that during the 1000-year reign of Christ the earth will be renovated and restored and that God's original purpose and design for this earth will be realized. But I also believe the Bible teaches that after the millennial reign of Christ, the present heaven and earth will be destroyed. Before the new heaven and new earth can be created, the present heaven and earth must be destroyed or at least dismantled. The old heaven and the old earth will disappear. This "end of the world" is mentioned several times in the Bible:

Psalm 102:25-26  "Of old You founded the earth, and the heavens are the work of Your hands. Even they will perish, but You endure; and all of them will wear out like a garment; like clothing You will change them and they will be changed."

Isaiah 34:4  "All the host of heaven will wear away, and the sky will be rolled up like a scroll; all their hosts will also wither away as a leaf withers from the vine, or as one withers from the fig tree."

Isaiah 51:6  "Lift up your eyes to the sky, then look to the earth beneath; for the sky will vanish like smoke, and the earth will wear out like a garment and its inhabitants will die in like manner; but My salvation will be forever, and My righteousness will not wane."

Matthew 24:35  "Heaven and earth will pass away."

2 Peter 3:10,12  "The day of the Lord will come like a thief, in which the heavens will pass away with a roar and the elements will be destroyed with intense heat,

and the earth and its works will be
burned up...the heavens will be
destroyed by burning, and the elements will melt with intense heat!"

Revelation 21:1    "The first heaven and first earth
passed away, and there is no longer
any sea."

The passing away of the present heaven and earth will occur right before the final judgment, according to Revelation 20:11: "I saw a great white throne and Him who sat upon it, from whose presence earth and heaven fled away, and no place was found for them." Just imagine what it will be like for all the people gathered at the Great White Throne Judgment: Right before they are judged by God and consigned to hell forever, the last thing they will behold is the entire universe going up in smoke. God will give them a final display of His power and show them the futility of all that they craved and cherished on this earth.

By the spoken word, God will simultaneously untie or break up every atom in the cosmos and the entire universe will dissolve and disintegrate in a fiery holocaust (2 Peter 3:7,10-13). This will be the ultimate fireworks show. After the present order is destroyed, God will put it all back together again. Like tearing down an old building and using the same materials to build it back again, the Lord will gather all the building blocks of the original creation and make a brand new universe that will exist for eternity.

## Long-term Perspective

In Scripture, teaching about the future is almost always followed by practical application of how the future should affect our lives today. In light of the coming end of the world, the apostle Peter urged us to live in the light of eternity and not simply for the here and now. "Since all these things are to be destroyed in this way, what sort of people ought you to be in holy conduct and godliness...Therefore, beloved, since you look for these things, be diligent to be found by Him in peace, spotless and blame- less" (2 Peter 3:11,14). It's the glorious hope of a better world to come that empowers and motivates God's people to live godly lives each day and enables them to handle the heartaches and disappointments of life here and now.

Speaking of the here and now, moving from the long term back to the short term, what signs, if any, are there that the events of the end times could be just over the horizon? If we're not to look for doomsday in 2012, what *are* we to look for?

# 11

# SCANNING THE HORIZON

### What 2 Look 4

"As students of Bible prophecy observe proper interpretation
principles, they are becoming increasingly aware of a remarkable
correspondence between the obvious trend of world events
and what the Bible predicted millennia ago."

JOHN F. WALVOORD

*(ARMAGEDDON, OIL AND THE MIDDLE EAST CRISIS)*

U nlike the self-proclaimed prophets of the past and present, Jesus and the biblical prophets did not peddle vague
and general predictions that could accommodate many different possible fulfillments. The prophecies recorded in the Bible are
detailed and intricately interwoven. The Bible does not simply
speak of the end of the world or doomsday, but of a whole series
of carefully timed events that are like signposts on the road to
Armageddon.

The final countdown in the Bible will involve years, not days.
Even before the countdown, the Bible predicts a number of pre-
liminary events that will set the stage for the political, economic,

and religious climate that is necessary for end-time events to occur. These preparatory events or steps appear to be falling into place in rapid succession. These are often referred to as "signs of the times."

## Discerning the Signs of the Times

Many people today react negatively to any mention of signs of the end times. They say it is foolish and unwarranted to look for or even talk about trends and developments that point toward the end-time scenario portrayed in Scripture. But is this negative outlook justified?

In Matthew 16:1-4, Jesus sternly rebuked the religious leaders of His day for their blindness to the signs of the times of His first coming.

> The Pharisees and Sadducees came up, and testing Jesus, they asked Him to show them a sign from heaven. But He replied to them, "When it is evening, you say, 'It will be fair weather, for the sky is red.' And in the morning, 'There will be a storm today, for the sky is red and threatening.' Do you know how to discern the appearance of the sky, but cannot discern the signs of the times?"

Jesus was fulfilling the Old Testament prophecies and performing the prophesied miracles of the Messiah right before their eyes, and yet they were blind to the clear signs of His first coming.

Likewise today, many religious leaders are following the same sad pattern of being blind to the things that are happening in the world in relation to God's program for the second coming of Christ.

A while back I was going out to jog for a couple of miles. I started by walking for a few minutes to get warmed up. As I walked along the sidewalk I noticed my shadow on the concrete in front of me. My shadow is not me, and it has no substance, but it signals that I am not far behind. It's a sign that I am coming. In the same way, coming events often cast their shadows upon this world before they arrive. These shadows function as signs of the times.

## Setting the Stage

Another illustration that helps explain what is meant by "the signs of the times" is this: Imagine you are at a play. You have taken your seat in the audience, and before the curtain goes up for Act One, you can hear sounds behind the curtain. The stage is being set for the beginning of the play. The props are being put in place and the actors are taking their positions. These events are not the play itself, but are a natural, necessary preparation for it. The setting of the stage creates anticipation for the parting of the curtain.

In the same way, God is preparing the world stage for His drama of the ages. The curtain is still shut. But behind the curtain, God is at work, putting the actors and props into place for when the drama begins. And before the curtain parts, all those who have trusted in Jesus Christ as their Savior will be raptured and meet the Lord in the air (1 Thessalonians 4:17).

Sometime after the rapture, the Antichrist will arrive on the world scene. At that point, all the pieces and players will be in place, ready to fulfill their roles in the final drama of the ages. This approach to understanding the signs of the times has often been referred to as "stage setting."

What are some of the signs today that indicate the Lord might return soon? We have already alluded to some of the signs earlier in this book. Let's briefly summarize them here.

### The Homecoming

After almost 1900 years in exile, near the beginning of the twentieth century, the Jewish people began to regather to their homeland, and the modern state of Israel was born on May 14, 1948. This "supersign" of the end times is the one critical piece to the puzzle that's necessary for the prophecies of the end times to be fulfilled.

### The Reuniting of the Roman Empire

The Bible predicts in Daniel chapters 2 and 7 and Revelation chapters 13 and 17 that the Roman Empire will be reunited in the end times. With half a billion people from 27 nations and a powerful currency (the Euro), the European Union could be the forerunner to this end-time superstate.

### World Focus on the Middle East

Fifty years ago, no one could have imagined that the Middle East would be the focus of the world. Yet today, with almost two-thirds of the world's proven oil reserves, radical Islam, and the Middle East crisis, this region is constantly front and center in the news. According to Scripture, the Middle East is the staging ground for the events of the end times, with Israel at the epicenter. World focus on the Middle East is another development that bears a remarkable correspondence to Bible prophecy.

### Globalism and the New World Order

Globalism is here. The 1990s were called the Decade of Globalization. But the move toward a global economy is now on fast-forward. The world is growing more interconnected every day. The global economic meltdown has heightened the call for more global interdependence. The New World Order is a phrase that we are hearing more and more from government leaders. The Bible predicts that in the end times there will be a one-world economy, government, and religion (Revelation 13). It looks like we are well on our way down that road.

### The Coming Middle East Peace

The Bible predicts that the seven-year Tribulation will begin with a peace treaty between the Antichrist and Israel (Daniel 9:27). What could be more relevant in today's world? The world is yearning for peace. The outcry has never been greater. Western powers are attempting to broker a Middle East peace deal and guarantee Israel's peace and security. The seemingly endless Middle East peace process points toward this end-time sign of the times.

### The Growing "Gog" Alliance

The prophet Ezekiel, writing 2500 years ago, predicted that an alliance of nations—including Russia, Iran, Turkey, Libya, and Sudan—will invade Israel in the end times (Ezekiel 38). All of these nations are currently strengthening their alliances with one another and all are Islamic, except Russia. These alliances are likely going to come into play in this coming invasion.

## A Word of Caution

It's important to bear in mind that the events we see today, other than the rebirth of the nation of Israel, are not yet the direct fulfillments of Bible prophecy. The curtain has not yet parted for the final act of God's great drama. But we can tell there is activity taking place behind the curtain. Presently, God is arranging the stage and putting the actors into place. Then God Himself will open the curtain when He raptures His people to heaven.

While it is helpful to evaluate headlines and current events in order to discern whether the end times are near, at the same time, we must be careful to remember that only God knows the future. We must always evaluate current events in light of the Bible, and never the other way around. There's always the danger of hyping every headline and sensationalizing every current event. This only serves to diminish credibility and can even cause people to turn away from true biblical prophecy and write it all off as nonsense.

Also, we need to remember that regardless of how much our present time may appear to fit the biblical template, there may be more stage-setting still to come.

## The Real Harmonic Convergence

Never before in human history has there been such a convergence of trends and developments that are part of the matrix of end-time events as predicted in Scripture. In 1948, the Jewish people re-established the nation of Israel. In 1957, the forerunner of the European Union, the EEC (European Economic Community), was founded. In the 1940s, the nuclear age was born. Nine nations currently have the bomb, and weapons of mass destruction are proliferating. For the last several decades, world attention has been riveted on the Middle East because of its oil, the never-ending Israeli-Palestinian crisis, and radical Islamic terror. The world today is clamoring for peace, especially in the Middle East; globalism and the New World Order are here; and the nations in Ezekiel 38–39 are nations we can identify today as having the will and desire to attack Israel.

All of this has come about in a time span of some 60 years! Is that mere coincidence? I don't think so. Viewed collectively, the impact of these signs is dramatic. The stage-setting today is accelerating so quickly we can hardly keep up. It's as if everything is on fast-forward. Emerging trends seem to pass us by before we even have time to understand them. Before we're able to catch our collective breath, we're hurried on to the next series of events on the horizon of the future.[1] We are well down the road toward the fulfillment of the prophecies of the end times. The coming of the Lord could be very soon.

The truth is that none of us know how much time we have *personally* or *prophetically*. Personally, we don't know if we will live to see tomorrow. God gives us no guarantee of another breath. Prophetically, Jesus could come today, and all who don't know Him as Savior will be left behind at the rapture. The signs of the end are all around us, and while many people are searching for answers, most people are ignoring God's warnings.

## The Final Stage Is Set

In 1974, John Walvoord, in his best-selling book *Armageddon, Oil and the Middle East Crisis,* wrote these words, which are more timely today than when he wrote them:

> The world is like a stage being set for a great drama. The major actors are already in the wings waiting for their moment in history. The main props are already in place. The prophetic play is about to begin. The Middle East today occupies the attention of world leaders. The world has now recognized the political and economic

power in the hands of those who control the tremendous oil reserves of the area. Old friendships and alliances will be subject to change as European nations seek new alliances and agreements to protect themselves in a changing world situation. The Middle East will continue to be the focal point of international relationships.

All the necessary historical developments have already taken place. The trend toward world government, begun with the United Nations in 1946, is preparing the way for the government of the end time.

Israel and the nations of the world have been prepared for the final drama. Most important, Israel is back in the land, organized as a political state, and eager for her role in the end-time events. Today Israel desperately needs the covenant of peace promised in prophecy. Largely because of the demands of the Palestinians, Israel will not be able to achieve a satisfactory settlement in direct negotiations.

Russia is poised to the north of the Holy Land for entry in the end-time conflict. Egypt and other African countries have not abandoned their desire to attack Israel from the south. Red China in the east is now a military power great enough to field an army as large as that described in the book of Revelation. Each nation is prepared to play out its role in the final hours of history.

Our present world is well prepared for the beginning of the prophetic drama that will lead to Armageddon. Since the stage is being set for this dramatic climax of the age, it must mean that Christ's coming for His own is very near. If there ever was an hour when men should consider their personal relationship to Jesus Christ, it is today. God is saying to this generation: "Prepare for the coming of the Lord."[2]

## Remember Harry Truman

In his book *Approaching Hoofbeats,* Billy Graham relates this fascinating story about the importance of heeding the warning signs God has given us.

No one who was around in 1980 can forget the explosion of Mt. Saint Helens. But many have forgotten Harry Truman, the man who failed to heed all the warning signs that had occurred over a period of many months. When Mt. Saint Helens was belching plumes of gray steam into the blue Washington sky, geologists alerted authorities of impending disaster. Sirens echoed up and down the mountain villages. Rangers and state police broadcast warnings from their patrol cars and helicopters. Tourists and residents were herded away from the ever-widening danger zone. But one man, Harry Truman, refused to budge.

Billy Graham describes what happened and what we should learn from Harry Truman:

> But Harry Truman refused to budge. Harry was the caretaker of a recreation lodge on Spirit Lake, five miles north of Mt. Saint Helens' smoke-enshrouded peak. The rangers warned Harry of the coming blast. Neighbors begged him to join them in their exodus. Even Harry's sister called to talk sense into the old man's head. But Harry ignored the warnings. From the picture-postcard beauty of his lakeside home reflecting the snow-capped peak overhead, Harry grinned on national television and said, "Nobody knows more about this mountain than Harry and it don't dare blow up on him..."
>
> On 18 May 1980, as the boiling gases beneath the mountain's surface bulged and buckled the landscape to its final limits, Harry Truman cooked his eggs and bacon, fed his sixteen cats the scraps, and began to

plant petunias around the border of his freshly mowed lawn. At 8:31 A.M. the mountain exploded...

Now Harry is a legend... He smiles down on us from posters and T-shirts and beer mugs. Balladeers sing a song about old Harry, the stubborn man who put his ear to the mountain but would not heed its warnings.[3]

Billy Graham concludes the story of Harry Truman with these thought-provoking words: "Maybe you are like ol' Harry Truman today. You see the warning signs all around you, yet you are ignoring them. You are going on with your life."[4]

This may describe you right now. You see the signs all around you, but you are trying to ignore them. You are going on with your life. If so, then the most important thing for you to do is to hear God's Word and be saved from the wrath to come.

# 2012 AND YOU

## Facing Your Future

"End dates are not the stuff of fantasy, after all; each and every one
of us has a terminal appointment inscribed in our calendars."

BENJAMIN ANASTAS (*THE NEW YORK TIMES*)

The timing of the end is in God's hands. From the human vantage point, it appears we are standing on the threshold of the final frontier. The pieces of the puzzle appear to be falling into place. The sands of time are rapidly slipping through the hourglass of eternity. The key questions for us are, "What should we do? And, what can we do in the meantime?"

In his well-researched, well-written book *Apocalypse 2012*, Lawrence E. Joseph ends with these words: "Don't be scared, be prepared."[1] While I disagree with much of what Joseph believes about 2012, I do agree with these words. We need to be prepared for the future. But how? What can we do to be ready for whatever comes?

## Look to Jesus

As we have seen, the Bible tells us what's going to happen to this world. And as important as that is, it is much more important to know what's going to happen to you when your life ends. This world as we know it has an expiration date. And every person does as well. None of us know how much time we have left. What will happen to you when the rapture comes, or when you die? You need to be very concerned about the future and your destiny if you are not a Christian.

Don't make the mistake of looking to political or even religious leaders for salvation. Look to Jesus Christ alone for salvation. Jesus is the only way to God. Jesus Himself said so: "I am the way, and the truth, and the life; no one comes to the Father but through Me" (John 14:6). Jesus presented Himself as the narrow gate that leads to life (Matthew 7:13) and as the only solid rock to build one's life upon (Matthew 7:24-25).

I recognize that in our increasingly pluralistic society, the statement that Jesus is the only way to God is offensive to many people. But again, we can know that Jesus' claims about Himself are true and trustworthy by remembering that He fulfilled hundreds of Old Testament prophecies and also predicted the future Himself with 100 percent accuracy. His deity is unquestionable. His works and words confirm it. Jesus is God in human flesh. Those who maintain there are many ways to God make a mockery out of His death on the cross. Jesus would not have come and paid the ultimate price if there was some other way to God. Why not believe God's Word and accept God's Son as your personal Savior?

What makes this matter so serious is that the time may be short. Everyone must decide what they will do with Jesus Christ.

He is God in human flesh. He entered human history born of a virgin, lived a sinless life, and was rejected by His generation. He came to die on the cross for the sins of the world. Jesus died on the cross for you to purchase a pardon for your sins. He rose the third day with a new, resurrected body. Christ ascended into heaven and will one day return to take those who believe in Him to Himself. Based on what Jesus did at the cross, God now offers a full and free pardon from the penalty of our sins. The Bible tells us that all have sinned (Romans 3:23). We are all separated from God because of sin. All that God requires is for you to receive His pardon by faith and accept Christ as your personal Savior. "As many as received Him, to them He gave the right to become children of God" (John 1:12).

Receiving Christ begins a walk of faith that never ends. When Christ comes at the rapture to take all who have accepted Him as Savior, He will take them out of this world. After that comes the Tribulation and ultimately, God's judgment. Once we understand this urgent message, we must lovingly communicate it to our families, friends, and everyone else we can. The headlines are screaming that the time is short. The communication of God's coming judgment is especially important in this generation that may witness the world's final hour.

## How Should We Then Live?

How should those who have received Christ live during what could be history's final days? Believers in the early church were consistently told to be on the lookout for the coming of Christ. They were also given clear, practical instruction about how they should live in light of this event. The most straightforward passage about this in the New Testament is 1 Peter 4:7-10:

> The end of all things is near; therefore, be of sound judgment and sober spirit for the purpose of prayer. Above all, keep fervent in your love for one another, because love covers a multitude of sins. Be hospitable to one another without complaint. As each one has received a special gift, employ it in serving one another as good stewards of the manifold grace of God.

Notice the word "therefore" in verse 7. Peter is saying to us "therefore," because the rapture could happen at any time, here's what you should be doing. This passage emphasizes four things Christians should do.

### 1. Keep your head clear *(maintain an active prayer life)*

As we approach the coming apocalypse, more and more people are going to get caught up in the prophetic frenzy. This is evident in the 2012 craze. People will be tempted to quit their jobs, sell all their possessions, and go wait on some mountaintop in their pajamas for Jesus to come or for the world to end on 12.21.12. But the Bible tells us that in view of the end of all things, we are to "be of sound judgment and sober spirit." We are to be sober-minded, clearheaded, mentally alert, and disciplined for the purpose of prayer, and not carried away by our emotions. Believing that the end of all things is at hand should spur us on to a sober, disciplined prayer life.

### 2. Keep your heart warm *(show love for others)*

The badge of Christianity is love (John 13:34-35). As we see the end approaching we are to "keep fervent in [our] love for one another." The word translated "fervent" means "to be stretched," and speaks of a runner whose muscles are stretched to the limit. Peter is saying that our love for one another is to be stretched out to the limit but never reaching the breaking point.

### 3. Keep your home open *(show hospitality to strangers)*

Jesus said that one of the signs of His second coming is that "most people's love will grow cold" (Matthew 24:12). In light of this fact, believers are called to show their love in a concrete way by reaching out in Christian love to strangers. This beautiful Christian virtue of hospitality is mentioned six times in the New Testament (Romans 12:13; 1 Timothy 3:2; 5:9-10; Titus 1:8; Hebrew 13:1-3; 1 Peter 4:9). As this world becomes a colder and colder and more isolating place, we are to keep our homes open and show the warmth of Christ to strangers.

### 4. Keep your hands busy *(use your spiritual gifts in service for the Lord)*

Every believer in Jesus Christ has at least one spiritual gift—that is, a supernatural, divine enablement and empowerment that God has given him or her to serve the church, the body of Christ (for a list of spiritual gifts, see 1 Corinthians 12:8-11,28-31; Romans 12:6-8). As we see the curtain about to open on the final act of history, the Lord is calling us to keep our hands busy, working in His service and using the gifts He has graciously given to us to build up one another and glorify Him.

## Ten Keys to Facing 2012 and Your Future

The world is speeding toward its ultimate date with destiny. Every day that passes moves us closer to the end. The planet has a divinely scheduled appointment to keep. Earth's final hour may be just around the corner. There will undoubtedly be many unexpected twists and turns as the clock of time ticks down to zero, but it's only a matter of time until the world is shocked by the rapture and plunged into the coming Tribulation.

As that time approaches and as the December 21, 2012 end-date continues to garner more and more attention, even fomenting hysteria and panic, it's important to hold onto a few very basic anchors. Here are ten anchors that can hold you firmly in place in these rapidly changing times:

1. Remember that God is in total control. He is the creator of the heavens and the earth. He alone knows the future. In the book of Revelation, the main prophetic name of God is "Almighty" (Greek, *Pantokrator*). This Greek word means to "hold everything in your hands" or to "have your hands on everything." God has His hands on everything. The words to the simple song really are true: "He's got the whole world in His hands." There's no need to be afraid of the future if you have trusted in the Lord. God has it all under control. As someone has aptly said, "History is *His*-story."

2. The world will not end on December 21, 2012. While the Mayans had incredible knowledge about our solar system and the universe, they could not accurately predict the future. No human can. The Mayans' prophecies were not based on divine revelation. And it's critical to remember that the Mayans themselves never said specifically that the world will end or that some new age will begin on December 21, 2012. Others have extrapolated this meaning from the ending of their calendar. The 2012ology that's flooding us from every direction is based on pure speculation and New Age mysticism.

3. Bible codes are of no value in predicting the time of the end and should not be consulted. God's message for us in the Bible is not hidden in mysterious codes. We are to read and accept what the Bible says on the surface and obey it.

4. Jesus will not return to earth for His second advent on December 21, 2012. Because the rapture has not yet occurred and the seven-year Tribulation (the final seven years of this age) has not yet begun, God's final seven-year countdown for the end of the age has not started.

5. We are living in the last days. This entire age between the two comings of Jesus Christ is the "last hour" (1 John 2:18) or the "last days" (Hebrews 1:1). There are no prophecies that must be fulfilled before Jesus can return for the rapture. And many events in our world, such as the return of the Jewish people to their land, indicate that we are closer to the end than ever before.

6. Some unusual things could happen on or near December 21, 2012. I don't know what they will be, but the alignment of the earth and sun with the galactic center of the Milky Way could cause some disturbances. Increased intensity in solar storms could cause disruptions. I'm no astronomer, physicist, or geologist. But whatever occurs, it won't bring about the end of the world, the mass extinction of humanity, or a quantum leap to a new level of human consciousness.

7. The rapture *could* happen in 2012. Remember, the rapture is a signless event, so it could happen in

2012 or any day before that time or after it. It's an
imminent event that could occur at any time. We
who are Christians are called to always be looking
for the coming of Christ. Not on some specific
day, but every day. If the rapture were to happen
in 2012, it would certainly cause quite a stir, and
some could misapply it to the whole 2012 phenomenon.

8. Avoid getting caught up in the speculation about
some great cosmic purification or universal expansion of consciousness that will come on December
21, 2012 or is already underway. Such teaching may
sound very attractive and persuasive in the midst
of our increasingly chaotic and dangerous world,
but it's simply the New Age movement version
2.0. Man's efforts alone have never and will never
bring in a golden age of peace and love. A simple
perusal of the news should make that clear. New
Age eschatology is man-centered and rejects God's
infallible revelation in the Bible.

9. Make sure you have trusted in Jesus Christ as
your Savior from sin. And do all you can to
spread the good news about Christ to others.

10. Don't panic or be drawn to carry out rash,
impulsive actions encouraged by fanatics and sur-
vivalists who claim to know the exact date of the
end of the world or Christ's coming. They don't
know when the world will end. Only God knows,
and He isn't telling anyone when it will happen.
As popular Bible teacher Warren Wiersbe said,
"God didn't give us prophecy to make calendars
but to build our character."[2] Commit yourself to

living a responsible, sober life for the Lord. Live as an ordinary person doing ordinary things, but do them with the extraordinary character of godliness, especially manifested in sincere love for others.

If you do these things, you will be ready to face the future.

# NOTES

## Chapter 1—12.21.12

1. David A. Patten, "Will He Return?" *Newsmax* (April 2009), 44.

2. Patten, "Will He Return?"

3. Patten, "Will He Return?"

4. Phil Johnson, "Apocalypse Then: Remembering the Y2K Hysteria" Pyromaniacs, January 5, 2009, http://teampyro.blogspot.com/2009/01/apocalypse-then.html#links.

5. Johnson, "Apocalypse Then: Remembering the Y2K Hysteria."

6. Lisa Miller, "2012: A Y2K for the New Age," *Newsweek* (May 11/May 18, 2009), 12.

7. Synthia Andrews and Colin Andrews, *The Complete Idiot's Guide to 2012* (New York: Alpha, 2008), 126.

8. Louis Sahagun, "Many gather to ponder end of Maya days," *Los Angeles Times,* November 3, 2008, articles.latimes.com/2008/nov/03/local/me-mayan3.

9. Sahagun, "Many gather to ponder end of Maya days."

10. "Thousands Expect Apocalypse in 2012," http://news.aol.com/story/_a/thousands-expect-apocalypse-in-2012/20080706152409990001.

11. Miller, "2012: A Y2K for the New Age."

12. Christine Brouwer, "Will the World End in 2012?" ABC News, July 3, 2008, abcnews.go.com/International/story?id=5301284&page=1.

13. "Thousands Expect Apocalypse in 2012."

14. Brouwer, "Will the World End in 2012?"

15. G. Jeffrey MacDonald, *USA Today* (March 27, 2007), http://usatoday.printthis.clickability.com/ptpcpt?action=cpt&title=Does+Maya+calendar+p.

16. Sahagun, "Many gather to ponder end of Maya days."

17. Reed Tucker, "2012: The End Is Nigh," January 25, 2009, www.nypost
    .com/seven/01252009/postopinion/postopbooks/2012_the_end_is_
    nigh_151704.htm.

18. Benjamin Anastas, "Apocalypse 2012," *U.S. News & World Report*
    (February-March 2008), 82-85.

19. Miller, "2012: A Y2K for the New Age."

20. A. Pawlowski, "Apocalypse in 2012? Date Spawns Theories, Film," CNN,
    January 27, 2009, www.cnn.com/2009/TECH/science/01/27/2012.maya
    .calendar.theories/index.html.

21. See December212012.com.

22. "Lil Wayne: The World Will End In 2012," May 14, 2008, www
    .starpulse.com/news/index.php/2008/05/14/lil_wayne_the_world_will_
    end_in_2012_.

23. James Montgomery, "Girl Talk Plans Apocalyptic 'Final' Show...For
    December 21, 2012," http://www.december212012.com/articles/news/
    Girl_Talk_Plans_Apocalyptic_Show.htm.

24. "Thousands of Dutch Prepare for 2012 Apocalypse, According to
    Report," Fox News, June 24, 2008.

25. Miller, "2012: A Y2K for the New Age."

**Chapter 2—An Ancient Doomsday Clock?**

1. José Arguelles, "The Mayan Factor," in *The Mystery of 2012: Predictions,
   Prophecies & Possibilities* (Boulder, CO: Sounds True, 2007), 73.

2. Daniel Pinchbeck, *2012: The Return of Quetzalcoatl* (New York: Penguin,
   2007), 1-2.

3. Gregg Braden, "Choice Point 2012," in *The Mystery of 2012: Predictions,
   Prophecies & Possibilities* (Boulder, CO: Sounds True, 2007), 1.

4. Gregg Braden, *Fractal Time: The Secret of 2012 and a New World Age*
   (Carlsbad, CA: Hay House, Inc., 2009), 69.

5. Synthia Andrews and Colin Andrews, *The Complete Idiot's Guide to 2012*
   (New York: Alpha, 2008), 11.

6. Andrews and Andrews, *The Complete Idiot's Guide to 2012.*

7. Andrews and Andrews, *The Complete Idiot's Guide to 2012,* 12.

8. Andrews and Andrews, *The Complete Idiot's Guide to 2012.*

9. Andrews and Andrews, *The Complete Idiot's Guide to 2012,* 13.

10. Lawrence E. Joseph, *Apocalypse 2012: An Investigation into Civilization's End* (New York: Broadway Books, 2007), 12.

11. Andrews and Andrews, *The Complete Idiot's Guide to 2012*, 42.

12. Andrews and Andrews, *The Complete Idiot's Guide to 2012*, 52.

13. Patricia Mercier, *The Maya End Times: A Spiritual Adventure; Maya Prophecies for 2012* (London: Watkins Publishing, 2008), 246.

14. Andrews and Andrews, *The Complete Idiot's Guide to 2012*, 79-80.

15. Braden, *Fractal Time*, 67.

16. Benjamin Anastas, "Apocalypse 2012," *U.S. News & World Report* (February-March 2008), 85.

17. Braden, *Fractal Time*, 154.

18. Andrews and Andrews, *The Complete Idiot's Guide to 2012*, 24.

19. Andrews and Andrews, *The Complete Idiot's Guide to 2012*, 35.

20. Andrews and Andrews, *The Complete Idiot's Guide to 2012*, 84.

21. Braden, *Fractal Time*, 67.

22. Andrews and Andrews, *The Complete Idiot's Guide to 2012*, 44.

23. Andrews and Andrews, *The Complete Idiot's Guide to 2012*, 7.

24. John Major Jenkins, *Maya Cosmogenesis 2012* (Rochester, VT: Bear & Company, 1998), 71.

25. Andrews and Andrews, *The Complete Idiot's Guide to 2012*, 46.

26. Geoff Stray, "The Advent of the Post-Human Geo-Neuron," in *The Mystery of 2012: Predictions, Prophecies & Possibilities* (Boulder, CO: Sounds True, 2007), 314.

27. Andrews and Andrews, *The Complete Idiot's Guide to 2012*, 46.

28. Jenkins, *Maya Cosmogenesis 2012*, 128. Jenkins provides an excellent, very detailed description and analysis of the cosmic symbolism of the Maya ballgame on pages 127-38.

29. Jenkins, *Maya Cosmogenesis 2012*, 132.

30. The Bible, in 1 Corinthians 8:4-6, tells us that idols are not real gods, but that "there is but one God, the Father, from whom are all things" (verse 6). However, it also reveals that there is a real power behind idols that is energized by demons (1 Corinthians 10:19-21).

31. John Major Jenkins, "The Origins of the 2012 Revolution," in *The Mystery of 2012: Predictions, Prophecies & Possibilities* (Boulder, CO: Sounds True, 2007), 40.

32. Anastas, "Apocalypse 2012," 85.

## Chapter 3—Apocalypse Now?

1. "Thousands Expect Apocalypse in 2012," July 6, 2008, news.aol.com/ story/_a/thousands-expect-apocalypse-in-2012/20080706152409990001; Gregg Braden, *Fractal Time: The Secret of 2012 and a New World Age* (Carlsbad, CA: Hay House, Inc., 2009), 57.

2. Lev Grossman, "Apocalypse New," *Time* (January 28, 2008), 211.

3. Reed Tucker, "2012: The End Is Nigh" (January 25, 2009),www.nypost .com/seven/01252009/postopinion/postopbooks/2012_the_end_is_ nigh_151704.htm.

4. Christine Brouwer, "Will the World End in 2012?" ABC News, (July 3, 2008), abcnews.go.com/International/story?id=5301284&page=1.

5. Lawrence Joseph develops a possible theory of how this information could have been communicated from Egypt to Mesoamerica, but his thesis is unproven. Lawrence E. Joseph, *Apocalypse 2012: An Investigation into Civilization's End* (New York: Broadway Books, 2007), 209.

6. Patrick Geryl, *How to Survive 2012: Tactics and Survival Places for the Coming Pole Shift* (Kempton, IL: Adventures Unlimited Press, 2007), 67.

7. Joseph, *Apocalypse 2012*, 58-72; Synthia Andrews and Colin Andrews, *The Complete Idiot's Guide to 2012* (New York: Alpha, 2008), 126-28, 300.

8. Geryl, *How to Survive 2012*, 68-71.

9. Geryl, *How to Survive 2012*, 71.

10. Patrick Geryl, *The World Cataclysm in 2012: The Maya Countdown to the End of Our World* (Kempton, IL: Adventures Unlimited Press, 2005), 9.

11. Joseph, *Apocalypse 2012*, 15.

12. Andrews and Andrews, *The Complete Idiot's Guide to 2012*, 123.

13. Joseph, *Apocalypse 2012*, 101, 114.

14. Tucker, "2012: The End Is Nigh."

15. Robert Roy Britt, "Powerful Solar Storm Could Shut Down U.S. for Months," January 9, 2009, www.foxnews.com/story/0,2933,478024,00 .html.

16. Britt, "Powerful Solar Storm."

17. Britt, "Powerful Solar Storm."

18. Ian O'Neill, "2012: No Killer Solar Flare," June 21, 2008, www .universetoday.com/2008/06/21/2012-no-killer-solar-flare.

19. Joseph, *Apocalypse 2012*, 160.

20. Tucker, "2012: The End Is Nigh."

21. Jacco van der Worp, Marshall Masters, and Janice Manning, *Planet X Forecast and 2012 Survival Guide* (Silver Springs, NV: Your Own World Books, 2007), xix.

22. "Planet X," www.2012warning.

23. Robert L. Thomas, *Revelation 1–7: An Exegetical Commentary* (Chicago: Moody Press, 1992), 453-54.

24. Geoff, Stray, *Catastrophe or Ecstacy: A Complete Guide to End-of-Time Predictions Beyond 2012* (East Sussek, UK: Vital Signs Publishing, 2006), 24.

25. Stray, *Catastrophe or Ecstacy.*

26. Stray, *Catastrophe or Ecstacy,* p. 76.

27. Gregg Braden, *Fractal Time: The Secret of 2012 and a New World Age* (Carlsbad, CA: Hay House, Inc., 2009), 175.

28. Ervin Laszlo, "The Birthing of a New World Order," in *The Mystery of 2012: Predictions, Prophecies & Possibilities* (Boulder, CO: Sounds True, 2007), 121.

29. Ed Hindson, *Final Signs: Amazing Prophecies of the End Times* (Eugene, OR: Harvest House, 1996), 64.

30. John Major Jenkins, *Maya Cosmogenesis 2012* (Rochester, VT: Bear & Company), XXXV.

31. Jenkins, *Maya Cosmogenesis 2012*, XL-XLI.

32. Lisa Miller, "2012: A Y2K for the New Age," *Newsweek* (May 11/May 18, 2009), 12.

33. Daniel Pinchbeck, *2012: The Return of Quetzalcoatl* (New York: Penguin, 2007), 1.

34. Pinchbeck, *2012: The Return of Quetzalcoatl,* 2.

35. Pinchbeck, *2012: The Return of Quetzalcoatl,* 2-3.

36. Pinchbeck, *2012: The Return of Quetzalcoatl,* 15.

37. Daniel Pinchbeck, "Meeting the Spirits," excerpt from *Toward 2012,* ed. Daniel Pinchbeck and Ken Jordan, February 6, 2009, www.nytimes .com/2009/02/06/books/chapters/chapter-toward-2012.html.

38. Hwee-Yong Jang, *The Gaia Project 2012: The Earth's Coming Great Changes* (Woodbury, MN: Llewellyn Publications, 2007), back cover.

39. Joseph, *Apocalypse 2012*, 32-33.

40. Joseph, *Apocalypse 2012*.

41. Joseph, *Apocalypse 2012*, 15.

42. James O'Dea, "You Were Born for Such a Time as This," in *The Mystery of 2012: Predictions, Prophecies & Possibilities* (Boulder, CO: Sounds True, 2007), 387.

43. Ian O'Neill, "No Doomsday in 2012" (May 19, 2008), www.universetoday.com/2008/05/19/no-doomsday-in-2012/.

44. Miller, "2012: A Y2K for the New Age."

45. See www.carlclegg.com/pillars/design.html.

## Chapter 4—The Lost Book of Nostradamus

1. As cited by Nostradamus Index, at www.sacred-texts.com/nos/.

2. Synthia Andrews and Colin Andrews, *The Complete Idiot's Guide to 2012* (New York: Alpha, 2008), 139.

3. Gregg Braden, *Fractal Time: The Secret of 2012 and a New World Age* (Carlsbad, CA: Hay House, Inc., 2009), 61.

4. My source for these translations is the Nostradamus index at www.sacred-texts.com/nos/, accessed January 21, 2009.

5. Tom Harris, "How Nostradamus Works," science.howstuffworks.com/nostradamus4.htm.

6. Many contemporary scholars reject the unity of the book and Isaiah's authorship of this section of the prophecy. They believe it was written by someone other than Isaiah after Cyrus had already risen by power. For a concise defense of the unity of Isaiah, see Geoffrey W. Grogan, "Isaiah," in Frank E. Gaebelein, gen. ed., *The Expositor's Bible Commentary*, vol. 6 (Grand Rapids: Zondervan, 1986), 6-11.

7. Tom Harris, "How Nostradamus Works."

8. "The Lost Book of Nostradamus," www.mendhak.com/40-the-lost-book-of-nostradamus.aspx.

## Chapter 5—Bible Codes, the Book of Revelation, and Armageddon

1. Gregg Braden, *Fractal Time: The Secret of 2012 and a New World Age* (Carlsbad, CA: Hay House, Inc., 2009), 181.

2. Lawrence E. Joseph, *Apocalypse 2012: An Investigation into Civilization's End* (New York: Broadway Books, 2007), 175.

3. Michael Drosnin, *The Bible Code* (New York: Touchstone, 1997), 13-14.

4. Richard A. Taylor, "Teaching Them [Wrong] Things," *The Journal of the Evangelical Theological Society* (December 2000), findarticles.com/p/articles/mi_qa3817/is_200012/ai_n8907588/.

5. Drosnin, *The Bible Code*, 1.

6. Drosnin, *The Bible Code*, 153-54.

7. Braden, *Fractal Time*, 120.

8. Mark Chalemin, *Deciphering the Bible Code* (Richardson, TX: Renewal Radio, 1998), 10.

9. *Newsweek* (June 9, 1997), 67.

10. "Bible Code," *The Skeptic's Dictionary* at www.skeptic.com/bibcode.html.

11. Taylor, "Teaching Them [Wrong] Things."

12. J. Paul Tanner, "Decoding the Bible Codes," *Bibliotheca Sacra* 157 (April–June 2000): 159.

13. Taylor, "Teaching Them [Wrong] Things."

14. Braden, *Fractal Time*, 118.

15. Braden, *Fractal Time*, 120.

16. Braden, *Fractal Time*, 120-21.

17. Braden, *Fractal Time*, 119.

18. Drosnin, *The Bible Code*, 123-27, 153.

19. Michael Drosnin, *Bible Code II: The Countdown* (New York: Viking, 2002), pp. 21,236.

20. Drosnin, *Bible Code II*, p. 235.

21. I say 19 judgments instead of 21 because the seventh seal contains the seventh trumpet, and the seventh trumpet contains the seven bowls of judgment.

22. Joseph, *Apocalypse 2012*, 178.

23. The Bible claims to be the inspired Word of God. The phrase, "Thus says the Lord" or similar phrases occur hundreds of times in the Old Testament. In the New Testament, 2 Timothy 3:16-17 and 2 Peter 2:19-21 affirm the doctrine of divine inspiration.

## Chapter 6—Computers and 2012

1. Chris Maxcer, "U.S. to Enlist 20-Petaflop IBM Supercomputer for Nuke Management Duty," *TechNewsWorld* (February 3, 2009), www.technewsworld.com/story/66067.html.

2. Synthia Andrews and Colin Andrews, *The Complete Idiot's Guide to 2012* (New York: Alpha, 2008), 161.

3. Andrews and Andrews, *The Complete Idiot's Guide to 2012*.

4. Ben Tremblay, "Web Bot—What is it? Can it predict stuff?" www.dailycommonsense.com/web-bot-what-is-it-can-it-predict-stuff/.

5. Andrews and Andrews, *The Complete Idiot's Guide to 2012*, 161.

6. Andrews and Andrews, *The Complete Idiot's Guide to 2012*.

7. Andrews and Andrews, *The Complete Idiot's Guide to 2012*, 162.

8. Tremblay, "Web Bot—What is it? Can it predict stuff?"

9. 2012 Predictions Review, 2012-predictions-review.blogspot.com/2008/01/webbot-project.html.

## Chapter 7—Does Anybody Really Know What Time It Is?

1. See www.bible.ca/pre-date-setters.htm.

2. "Apocalypse now? 30 days when the world didn't end," TimesOnline, September 9, 2008," http://www.timesonline.co.uk/tol/comment/faith/article4717864.ece?token=null&offset=0&page=1.

3. Ed Hindson, *Final Signs: Amazing Prophecies of the End Times* (Eugene, OR: Harvest House, 1996), 191. Much of the material in this section has been adapted from this book.

4. Hindson, *Final Signs*, 196.

## Chapter 8—Can Anyone Know the Future?

1. Nancy Gibbs, "Apocalypse Now," *Time* (July 1, 2002), 42-48.

2. John F. Walvoord, "The Rapture: The Next Event on God's Calendar," in *The Road to Armageddon* (Nashville: Word, 1999), 29-30.

3. Randall Price, *Jerusalem in Prophecy* (Eugene, OR: Harvest House, 1988), 32-33.

4. This information and illustration are originally from Peter Stoner, who is referenced by Josh McDowell in his classic *Evidence that Demands a Verdict* (see http://www.bible-prophecy.com/fulfilled.htm).

## Chapter 9—Future Tense

1. Benjamin Anastas, "The Final Days," *The New York Times* (July 1, 2007), http://www.nytimes.com/2007/07/01/magazine/01world-t.html?.

2. Anastas, "The Final Days."

3. For an excellent presentation of the 70 weeks' prophecy see Harold Hoehner, *Chronological Aspects of the Life of Christ* (Grand Rapids: Zondervan, 1975).

4. Gregg Braden, *Fractal Time: The Secret of 2012 and a New World Age* (Carlsbad, CA: Hay House, Inc., 2009), 191.

5. This view is known as *premillennialism.* There are four key arguments that support the premillennial position—that is, taking the 1000 years as a literal, future period of time.

    1. The phrases "and I saw" and "then I saw" (19:11,17,19; 20:1,4,11; 21:1) appear 32 times in the book and indicate that what is described is sequential and follows the second coming of Christ in Revelation 19.

    2. The phrase "thousand years" is mentioned six times in Revelation 20:1-6. Time periods that are repeated over and over again in Revelation ("time, times, and half a time," "42 months," "1260 days") are always literal, so we should take "thousand years" to be literal.

    3. The nonspecific references "a short time" (20:3) and "like the sand of the seashore" (20:8) in the very same context support taking the phrase "thousand years" literally.

    4. This was the view of the early church. Early luminaries such as Papias (A.D. 60–130), Justin Martyr (100–165), Irenaeus (130–202), Tertullian (160–230), and Victorinus (d. 304) held to a literal, earthly 1000-year kingdom that follows the second coming of Christ. They were called *chiliasts,* from the Greek word for thousand (*chilias*). Tyconius and Augustine departed from this position in about 400.

6. In the Old Testament, false prophets frequently twisted God's message or outright contradicted what the Lord had said about the future, often for financial gain or popularity (1 Kings 22:13-24; Micah 3:5-8). In 2 Thessalonians 2:1-3 we discover that false teachers, in contradiction to the apostle Paul, taught that the end times ("the day of the Lord")

had already arrived. This unsettled and disturbed the new believers in Thessalonica. Paul wrote 2 Thessalonians 2:3-12 to clear up the issue.

7. These 20 prophecies were adapted from John F. Walvoord, *Prophecy Knowledge Handbook* (Wheaton, IL: Victor Books).

## Chapter 10—In the End, God

1. Randy Alcorn, *Heaven* (Wheaton, IL: Tyndale House, 2004), 87-98.

## Chapter 11—Scanning the Horizon

1. Ed Hindson, *Earth's Final Hour: Are We Really Running Out of Time?* (Eugene, OR: Harvest House, 1999), 9.

2. John F. Walvoord, *Armageddon, Oil and the Middle East Crisis,* rev. ed. (Grand Rapids: Zondervan, 1990), 228.

3. Billy Graham, *Approaching Hoofbeats: The Four Horsemen of the Apocalypse* (Waco, TX: Word Books, 1983), 13-14.

4. Graham, *Approaching Hoofbeats,* 14.

## Chapter 12—2012 and You

1. Lawrence E. Joseph, *Apocalypse 2012: An Investigation into Civilization's End* (New York: Broadway Books, 2007), 236.

2. Warren W. Wiersbe, *The Bible Exposition Commentary,* vol. 2 (Wheaton, IL: Victor Books, 1989), 196.

*Also by Mark Hitchcock*

## When the World Goes Cashless, the Antichrist Isn't Far Behind

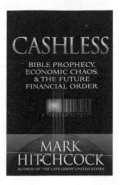

Over 1900 years ago, the Bible predicted that one man, the coming Antichrist, will take control of the entire world's economy. Many have wondered how this could ever happen. We may now have the answer.

Today's worldwide financial chaos, global interdependency, and modern technology are all converging in such a way that a cashless society and one-world economy are not only possible, but inevitable.

Bestselling author Mark Hitchcock skillfully brings together current research and Bible prophecy as he addresses these important questions:

- How is the stage being set for a cashless society?
- What technology will make this cashless world possible?
- How will the Antichrist control the world economy?
- What is the mark of the beast?
- What is the significance of the number 666?

And most important of all: Are you prepared?